PRAISE FOR *ORDINARY MIND*

"Deeply humane and broadly informed, *Ordinary Mind* is a gracefully written, persistently modest account of the way Magid has combined his analytic and meditation practices. The result is challenging, accessible, and sometimes wryly witty—a lovely and moving book."
—Prof. Susan Oyama, Emerita,
John Jay College, author of Evolution's Eye

"Readily accessible to a layperson, yet replete with penetrating analysis and insight that make it worthy of serious attention by the scholar, this is a profound book. With its subtle criticisms and erudite prescriptions, *Ordinary Mind* shows us the limits and possibilities of Zen and psychoanalysis—both as fully human endeavors. Dr. Magid has offered us a remarkable work."
—Prof. David Fryer, Illinois Wesleyan University

"This is a groundbreaking book. Magid's treatment of the subject is—at long last!—neither superficial nor based on long-obsolete theoretical formulations, but makes careful use of truly contemporary psychoanalytic thought. The ways in which he relates Zen practice to clinical issues is masterful. Zen students and mental-health professionals alike will be in his debt for a long time to come."
—John Daishin Buksbazen,
Faculty, Southern California Psychoanalytic Institute,
author of Zen Meditation in Plain English

ORDINARY MIND

ORDINARY MIND

EXPLORING THE COMMON GROUND
OF ZEN AND PSYCHOTHERAPY

Barry Magid

WISDOM PUBLICATIONS • BOSTON

Wisdom Publications
199 Elm Street
Somerville, MA 02144 USA
www.wisdompubs.org

Library of Congress Cataloging-in-Publication Data
Magid, Barry
    Ordinary mind : exploring the common ground of Zen and psychotherapy /
      Barry Magid.
      p. cm.
    Includes bibliographical references and index.
    ISBN 0-86171-306-0
    1. Religious life—Zen Buddhism. 2. Psychotherapy—Religious aspects—
      Zen Buddhism. 3. Buddhism and psychoanalysis. I. Title.

    BQ9286.M34 2001
    294.3'375—dc21   2001046776

07 06 05 04 03 02
6 5 4 3 2 1

Earlier versions of portions of this book appeared as "The Couch and the Cushion: Integrating Zen and Psychoanalysis," *Journal of the American Academy of Psychoanalysis* (fall 2000); "Baseball and the Mind/Body Problem," *Academy Forum* (fall 1992).

Excerpts from *The Gateless Barrier: The Wu-Men Kuan (Mumonkan) Translated and with a Commentary by Robert Aitken.* Copyright 1991 by the Diamond Sangha. Reprinted by permission of North Point Press, a division of Farrar, Straus and Giroux, LLC.

Jacket design by Laura Shaw Feit
Interior design by Gopa & Ted2
Jacket photograph by Aaron Siskind, from the Robert Mann Gallery

Printed in Canada

To my teachers,

Charlotte, Sharon, and Sam

CONTENTS

Foreword by Charlotte Joko Beck   IX

Acknowledgments   XIII

Introduction   1

Chapter 1. The Psychology of the Self   13

Chapter 2. Top-Down Practice: Mu   25
    Chao-chou's Dog   30

Chapter 3. Bottom-Up Practice: Just Sitting   35
    The Goose in the Bottle 40

Chapter 4. Self and Oneness   43
    Sung-yüan's Person of Great Strength 52

Chapter 5. Self and Emptiness   55
    Hsi-chung Builds Carts 59

Chapter 6. No Self   63
    Dogen's Encouraging Words 73

Chapter 7. The Myth of the Isolated Mind   77

    Jui-yen Calls "Master"   84

Chapter 8. Constancy   87

    Nan-ch'üan Kills the Cat   96

Chapter 9. Change   101

    Sitting with Sam   112

Chapter 10. Zen Is Useless   115

    "Wash Your Bowl"   125

Chapter 11. Relationship and Authority   129

    Attachment and Detachment   140

Chapter 12. One Practice or Two?   143

    What Shakes Your Tree?   155

Chapter 13. Form and No Form   159

    "Ordinary Mind Is the Tao"   164

Notes   169

Glossary   177

References   181

Index   185

About the Author   191

FOREWORD

IF ASKED what we would like our life to be, many of us might answer something like: "I would like my life to be sane and fruitful." Some of us might also add that we would like it to be satisfying and of benefit to others. This is all well and good! But for most of us, our life is not actually like that, and we are confused about why this is the case, why we can't achieve what we want from our life.

There are lots of ways to try to get what we want. Psychotherapy is often one of the things we try. Indeed, it is often very useful—and yet, psychotherapy often falls short of leading us completely to a satisfying life. As a Zen teacher, I hear my students say over and over statements like, "I've been in therapy for fifteen years, and I've learned much that has helped me—but still something is missing. I still have no real freedom." Often the students who say this are themselves therapists (at any given time, I have thirty to forty students who are therapists). They tell me that just being at ease with their life continues to elude them.

When anyone asks me what Zen practice has to offer, I answer, "Nothing." I never give advice and I never promise a solution. Any new student is simply asked to do his best with a few simple instructions involving awareness. This awareness spans a few areas. First, we have to be clear about what we're doing—and not doing—during meditation, during *zazen*. We need to learn to observe and label our thoughts and to fully experience our body and all its tensions and sensations as we sit. Next, everyday life, and the problems that surface in it, needs to be experienced as constant practice; this is difficult and demanding work, especially in the early years of practice. Over time and very slowly, the student sees that the "answers" to her life—a life that is sane and fruitful—don't lie in some mystical la-la land but in her own mind and body, her own direct experience.

As Zen practice continues, as the student builds courage and determination, she notices that the inherent dualism of a "me" looking at "problems" needs to be questioned. The ceaseless (and futile!) efforts to "fix" oneself and others fade as it becomes obvious that fixing is simply not the answer to human difficulties. When this happens, a person begins to comprehend the crucial difference between "fixing" and "transforming."

But it is very hard, if not impossible, to convey with words the difference between a life that is fixed and one that is transformed. For one thing, there is a blazing physicality in Zen practice that is obvious only within the silence and struggle of zazen. In experiencing without thoughts the bodily tension of emotion, the conditioned self or shell begins to weaken, and the possibility of the satisfying life we all want—the *transformed* life—begins to be born. A Zen teacher will make it clear to the student when she is not staying with reality, with what's happening right now, but is instead persisting in trying to find a solution based on self-centered, blaming thinking.

Zen practice can be difficult, frustrating, and slow, but after a time (usually a long time) the student will notice that her emotional reactivity is decreasing and that the ability to act clearly and sanely is increasing. Self-centeredness diminishes, as does being judgmental. Relationships are more intimate and more satisfying. Compassion appears more frequently and is effortless.

But this practice is a lifetime work and is never done. It is a process of experiencing again and again each thing that enters our life, moment by moment.

Good therapy and Zen practice can both do much to uncover the painful and hidden material of our lives. How they tend to differ is in how they deal with what is uncovered. A therapist who is a Zen practitioner will handle this material, both in himself and in his work with his clients, very differently than he would before he began doing Zen practice. Frequently, my students who are therapists tell me about the differences in the way they now approach their work; it is quite moving to them and to me when genuine transformation begins to replace all those futile attempts at helping and fixing.

The organic process of transformation changes everything we do, but it is not a change through our own efforts. It is just life happening through mind and body. And while it is always surprising and powerful and wonderful, it is also very ordinary—as ordinary as scrubbing carrots.

Barry Magid clearly brings this transformed perspective from his own Zen practice and Zen teaching into the way he does psychotherapy. *Ordinary Mind* is an excellent discussion of a vital matter. I sincerely hope that therapists especially will read it with care and consideration, for their own sakes and for the contribution it can make to the lives of their clients. Everyone, whether in therapy or not, can learn much here about the true cause and the true end of suffering, and the way of fully experiencing our life as it is.

Charlotte Joko Beck
San Diego, California

ACKNOWLEDGMENTS

I would like to thank all those whose conversation and comments on earlier versions of this work and the themes I have tried to address here have proved so valuable in bringing this book to completion, especially: George Atwood, Joseph Bobrow, Sharon Dolin, Lou Nordstrom, Pauline Pinto, Phil Ringstrom, Jeffrey Rubin, and Jeremy Safran. I also wish to thank all the members of the Ordinary Mind sangha who offered their reflections on their own experience of integrating their therapy with Zen practice, and whose ongoing commitment to practice has made the Zendo a reality. Finally, I wish to thank my editor, Josh Bartok, for his close, insightful reading of my manuscript, his invaluable suggestions, and his ongoing support for this project.

INTRODUCTION

FOR THE PAST twenty-five years I have been practicing both psychoanalysis and Zen Buddhism: at first as a patient in my own analysis when I was a beginning Zen student, and now as a psychoanalyst and Zen teacher myself. In the early days, it felt like I was conducting two separate practices in parallel, and I often wondered how they could, or should, relate to one another. As the years passed, however, they have increasingly converged, and I have begun to see both of them as structured disciplines of moment-to-moment awareness. Gradually, I evolved a common conceptual framework to describe the mechanism of character change within both. What I learned in analysis informed what I saw taking place in the *zendo,* just as the changes I saw happen in myself and others through Zen practice made me rethink some of my basic ideas about what brings about therapeutic change.

The convergence of these seemingly very different practices in my own life reflects, I believe, an evolution in how our society views meditation. Practices that were once seen as purely religious or spiritual have taken on a quasi-therapeutic aspect in the public eye and attract people for the same reasons they might consider entering psychoanalytic therapy. As economic forces push psychotherapy more and more toward a medical model—and as managed care mandates specific diagnoses, symptom-focused treatment plans, and psychopharmacological solutions—spiritual practices of all kinds now address issues of identity, quality of life, well-being, and the role of values in contemporary life—questions that people once entered psychoanalysis to address. More and more of my patients have had some interest in, or experience of, some form of spiritual practice, whether yoga, meditation, martial arts, or some New Age hybrid. The same holds true for many of my professional colleagues, many of whom currently augment whatever they originally sought and learned through psychoanalytic therapy with a personal spiritual practice of some sort—one that they may only vaguely know how to relate to what goes in the therapy they practice with their patients. Likewise, many of my Zen students have been in some form of therapy. But while more and more individuals seek to combine a variety of practices within their own lives, they often feel a certain unease about how these different practices relate to each other conceptually. Is meditation merely an escape from psychological problems? Does a psychological approach to meditation reduce spirituality to self-help? Might it not be best to keep the practices separate, let each work in its own sphere, and not worry too much about what the methods and results of one imply for the other?

But both psychoanalysis and Buddhism attempt to offer a comprehensive model of the mind and a mode of dealing with human suffering. Can two systems of thought that address the same set of problems really be incommensurable? Shouldn't we be able to find some common ground on which to build a dialogue that allows each to challenge and stimulate the other? What might convince a Buddhist teacher and a psychoanalyst that they have something to gain from such a dialogue?

Roughly fifty or sixty years ago, Zen and psychoanalysis went through another period of convergence, one that has been memorialized in a collection of essays by Erich Fromm, D.T. Suzuki, and Richard de Martino. That collection grew out of a conference in Cuernavaca Mexico in 1957 sponsored by the Department of

Psychoanalysis of the Medical School of the Autonomous National University of Mexico, attended by about fifty psychiatrists and psychologists, the majority of whom were psychoanalysts. The impetus behind the conference came from some of the most prominent and innovative thinkers in the analytic community, including Erich Fromm and Karen Horney. These psychoanalysts, struggling to articulate an alternative to classical psychoanalytic theory, found in Zen a compelling method of radical personality change that seemed to operate on wholly different principles than those of Freud's standard model. For Fromm, the crucial step was to move from a psychology of illness to a new psychology of well-being, which he called "humanistic" psychoanalysis:

> If we stay within the Freudian system, well-being would have to be defined in terms of libido theory, as the capacity for full genital functioning, or from a different angle as an awareness of the hidden Oedipal situation, definitions of which, in my opinion, are only tangential to the real problem of human existence and the achievement of well-being by the total man. Any attempt to give a tentative answer to the problem of well-being must transcend the Freudian frame of reference and lead to a discussion, incomplete as it must be, of the basic concept of human existence, which underlies humanistic psychoanalysis.

Zen offered that generation of analysts what appeared to them to be valuable new data about the nature of insight and human potentiality, data that could not be accounted for from within the Freudian paradigm and that could thus serve an important impetus for system building and paradigm change within psychoanalysis.

Today, the field of psychoanalysis is in very different shape. The Freudian hegemony has been overthrown, and pluralism is the order of the day. Schools of self psychology, intersubjectivity, and relational psychology are thriving. Fromm's battle to open up psychoanalysis to non-Freudian ways of thinking has been won. But that victory has meant that there is little current impetus to come to terms with Buddhist psychology; Western psychology is doing just fine now, thank you, thus the incentive has come not from theoretical tensions within the field, as in Fromm's day, but, we might say, from tensions within the analysts themselves, many of whom turn to meditation as often as further analysis, for help in dealing with the stresses and strains of modern life or their profession. At the same time, psychoanalysis faces increasing competition from Eastern practices in the search for meaning in life. Increasing numbers of people who cannot name a single contemporary psychoanalyst are familiar with the Dalai Lama and his teachings on happiness and compassion.

Having received my initial psychoanalytic training from teachers and supervisors who trained with Karen Horney and her followers, I was exposed from the start to a humanistic and existentialist brand of psychoanalysis, one that was conducive to my ongoing interest in Zen practice. In those early years of my training—back in the mid-seventies—I went three times a week to my analyst and three times a week to the zendo. In 1996, after twenty years of Zen practice, my current teacher, Charlotte Joko Beck, formally gave me permission to begin teaching Zen myself, and I opened the Ordinary Mind Zendo in a space adjacent to my psychoanalytic office. Since then, a number of current and former analysands have joined a few others for weekly group meditations and regular intensive *sesshins*.

In this book I will give an account of Zen practice that is informed by my own psychoanalytic perspective from within self psychology and intersubjectivity. These new schools of psychoanalytic thought, along with others offering a relational model, have answered Fromm's call for a non-Freudian approach that acknowledges the centrality of the search for meaning and does not reduce issues of identity and motivation to modes of coping with irrational drives. From within these new perspectives, we are now in a much better position to understand the hitherto problematic Zen ideas of oneness, emptiness, no-self, and enlightenment and to explore how these concepts and the experiences can make sense within a psychoanalytic model of the mind. I hope to demonstrate that Zen and psychoanalysis can be understood within a conceptually unified picture of the self and of practice. Indeed, as a symbol of the integration I believe is possible, throughout this book I will use the word *practice* to encompass what goes on in both psychoanalysis and Zen meditation. Whether working with an analyst or a teacher, whether on the couch or on the cushion, what we most fundamentally are practicing is attention, awareness of the moment-by-moment unfolding of our thoughts and feelings. If we can develop a common language to describe what that unfolding teaches us, as we sit in meditation or converse with our analyst, perhaps we can begin to assess the benefits and pitfalls associated with each practice.

And yet, the form and character of the two practices will remain different. I don't imagine, and I am certainly not proposing, that the two merge and lose their distinctive qualities. Perhaps, to borrow a line from the *Sandokai*, they can proceed together "like one foot forward and the other behind in walking." In what follows, speaking as a psychoanalyst, I will try to provide a coherent, psychoanalytic frame of reference within which to understand what goes on in Zen practice. In alternating sections I will speak more directly as a Zen teacher, either in the informal style of my weekly Dharma talks or in the more traditional and formal style of the talks I give during sesshins. The latter take the form of comments on cases from

The Gateless Barrier, a collection of koans assembled by thirteenth-century Chinese Zen master Wu-men, or on passages from the classic text of Japanese Soto Zen, Master Dogen's *Shobogenzo,* which dates from roughly the same period.

Although at times (or to different readers), I imagine these two voices may sound very different, I hope, as the book proceeds, they will complement one another or even blur together. Other voices too will find their place in what follows; I am not just a psychoanalyst and a Zen teacher but a father and husband too. One lesson of Zen is that there is no one thing that we "really" are.

This account necessarily reflects the vantage point my own lineage, both my psychoanalytic lineage as a follower of Heinz Kohut, the founder of self psychology, and my Zen lineage as a Dharma successor to Charlotte Joko Beck, who established her own Ordinary Mind school of Zen. In the chapters that follow I will try to show what has made Kohut and Beck such distinctive figures within contemporary psychoanalysis and Zen. Of course, it is possible that my view of their uniqueness is skewed by the importance they have had in my own life. Other therapists and Buddhist practitioners have no doubt arrived at very different versions of integration, while still other therapists and teachers emphasize what they see as the irreconcilable differences between Eastern religion and Western science. I make no claims that what follows is the best or only way to conceptualize the relationship between Zen and psychotherapy. I simply offer it as a model that has worked in my own life and practice.

If the initial impulse for a dialogue between Zen and psychoanalysis came from within psychoanalysis, nowadays there are Buddhist teachers of all persuasions trying to come to terms with Western psychology, both to understand their students better and to discover how Buddhist practice can best connect to the problems of modern life. But on the surface, Zen seems to be a wholly different sort of discipline from psychoanalysis, one that makes very different and particularly intense demands on its students. How should we understand the function of those demands from a psychoanalytic point of view? And what, in turn, can a psychoanalytic perspective tell us about how Zen works, who it works for, who it fails, and why?

Zen practice is hard, both emotionally and physically. In addition to a regular daily meditation practice, Zen students traditionally attend intensive week-long sesshins, which demand twelve or more hours a day of often painful motionless sitting. Clearly, the rigors of Zen should not be confused with any sort of relaxation technique or meditation that aims at simply quieting the mind or becoming calm. Often the sheer physical difficulty of Zen practice has been emphasized as what sets it apart from other meditation practices, as much as its storied promise of sudden great enlightenment or *kensho*. The beginning student may not have a clue as to what enlightenment really means, but he or she all too quickly learns what it means to sit with excruciatingly painful knees. Mastering one's reaction to pain may be the new student's first challenge, as if Zen were primarily a matter of cultivating toughness and endurance. Just learning to survive a sesshin can lead to a not-so-subtle elitism and pride in one's capacity to handle the pains or challenges that life throws our way—not an inconsiderable accomplishment, to be sure, but one that would seem on the surface to have more in common with the marines than with psychoanalysis.

I vividly remember a Japanese Rinzai Zen teacher recounting to his assembled students the parable of the mother tiger and her cubs. The mother tiger, he said, throws all her cubs off a steep cliff when they are only a few weeks old. She will raise only those cubs that are strong enough to scramble back up the slope on their own. The rest are left to die at the base of the cliff. "Which kind of cub are you?" he growled. Not being samurai material myself, I was pretty sure I knew the answer to that one.

My own version of psychoanalytic Zen, therefore, has set up shop at the base of that cliff, ministering to those abandoned cubs, each according to its own needs. That Japanese teacher undoubtedly taught a valuable, rigorous, authentic Zen, one that had no qualms about its elitism and that contained a not-too-subtle contempt for those who couldn't keep up. Ironically, that same teacher later became embroiled in a series of scandals precipitated by his repeated sexual advances to his female students. Sadly, there seemed to be no avenue within his brand of teaching to acknowledge and work through his own personal weaknesses. He was, unfortunately, not an isolated example. The recurring inability of many teachers from a broad variety of spiritual disciplines to deal appropriately with the eroticized longings of their students—and with the emotional reactions and temptations that arise in the teachers themselves as a result—has been one of the main sources of a growing appreciation in Buddhist communities for psychoanalytic training and the experience it brings to meditation practice.

It is the explicit acknowledgment and working through of the *emotional* difficulties of practice that has been the hallmark of Joko Beck's distinctive brand of Zen. Her way of practicing and teaching was born directly out of the failure of so many of the first generation of Japanese and American teachers here in the United States to adequately deal with their own emotional conflicts, transference reactions, substance abuse, and sexual behavior despite having completed traditional Zen training. Janwillem van de Wetering's memoir *Afterzen,* an insider's account of Rinzai training and koan study, recounts, often quite comically, the slew of emotional difficulties that dogged (and sometimes ruined) the lives of "enlightened" teachers, dedicated monks, and devoted lay students alike. Jeffrey Rubin and Michael Eigen, analysts with strong sympathies for meditation practice, are among those who have documented case after case of experienced meditators whose core conflicts and deficits have not only been inadequately addressed through their practice, but for whom meditation itself served to reinforce defensive patterns. Too often, it seems that both students and teachers have mastered their physical pain but succumbed to their impulses, experienced a oneness with all beings but remained in conflict with their families, discovered the emptiness of self but continued to abuse their authority—in short, found peace on their cushions but not in their lives.

It is my hope that an understanding of transference and an appreciation for the role of empathy can transform the traditional student/teacher relationship. Transference is a broad term used by analysts to encompass the whole range of emotional and relational reactions between the analyst and patient. It includes both the forward- and backward-looking expectations that we bring to new relationships. On the one hand, we are hopeful and expectant. We look forward to being understood and responded to in a way that we may have missed while growing up. We long to encounter someone whom we can admire and who, in turn, will appreciate our own uniqueness. On the other hand, we also bring the memories of old disappointments and emotional traumas into each new situation. We all have devised defensive postures to insure that no one will ever do *that* to us again. It is part of the analyst's training and expertise to learn to recognize the ever-shifting, subtle patterns of longing and defensiveness that emerge in the course of therapy. It is also part of the analyst's training to remain aware of all the emotions he or she feels as a result of being the focus of all these supercharged expectations. Wildly idealized as a savior one day only to be fiercely abused as a betrayer of confidences the next, even a well-seasoned therapist can suffer emotional whiplash.

Good Buddhist teachers of all persuasions, of course, operate with an intuitive feeling for their students' emotional needs and reactions, but they may vary in their capacity to understand and effectively deal with intense idealizations, eroticized longings for father figures, or the disappointment, rage, or withdrawal that can accompany the disruption of fantasies and expectations. Even experienced teachers may underestimate the extent to which an apparently devoted student may form a morbid dependency on the teacher. Such students make what analysts call a *pathological accommodation* and spend years stuck in a role of compliance, masochistically enduring a painful training solely to maintain a tie to an idealized role model. Coping with being the object of students' idealization, especially when it is erotically charged, has proven to be an ongoing challenge for many teachers. I hope we are entering a time when teachers are able to turn to psychotherapy as a way of dealing with their own unexpected emotional needs and reactions— *before* a crisis forces the issue. And likewise I hope that empathy and a psychoanalytically based understanding of transference reactions can enable teachers to understand and respect the differing emotional needs, weaknesses, and strengths of different students, rather than imposing a one-size-fits-all discipline.

For example, a student once came to me to discuss an impasse that had arisen with his teacher. Although he had studied with this teacher for over a decade, both he and the teacher had concluded he could no longer be that teacher's student. The student explained to me that in recent years (he was now in his forties) his back had started giving him trouble. He found it increasingly difficult to do the full bows that were part of the Buddhist service and that were also done for extended periods of "bowing practice." After his last sesshin, he had been laid up for several days with back spasms. He therefore asked his teacher to be excused from this practice, fully expecting him to understand his problem. However, the teacher told him he had to do the bows. Everyone has one kind of difficulty or another, his teacher said, including physical pain. If his back hurt, that was simply something he had to practice with.

This response shattered the student's relationship with his teacher. Suddenly the teacher reminded him of his cold, perfectionistic father, who never took the time to understand his problems. Aware of the transferential aspect of his reaction, he attempted to explain to the teacher the old feelings and memories that the teacher's words had stirred up in him. But the teacher brushed all that aside, saying that was the past; Zen meant staying in the present. The teacher evidently felt that the student needed to practice staying in the present moment as a way to erase the past associations; the student felt there was no point in arbitrarily suffering just to satisfy some unbending, impersonal rule. If the teacher couldn't understand that, where was his compassion? To stay with his teacher felt like a masochistic form of compliance, and compliance seemed to be the requirement the teacher placed on him to continue their relationship.

In this case, one might say that the teacher was perfectly correct in everything he said—except none of it was of any use to this particular student. (It's always easier to be right than to be helpful.) Unfortunately, a long productive relationship was sacrificed when the student was unable to conform to a one-size-fits-all approach. The teacher would say the student simply encountered a barrier of self-centeredness he was unable to break through. Many students continue to profit from this teacher's uncompromising approach. But what about the others?

CHAPTER ONE

THE PSYCHOLOGY
OF THE SELF

JUST A FEW MONTHS after Erich Fromm's historic meeting with D.T. Suzuki in Mexico in 1957, an analyst named Heinz Kohut delivered a paper to the Chicago Institute for Psychoanalysis that would quietly initiate a revolution within classical Freudian psychoanalysis. Not all psychoanalytic revolutions began so quietly. In 1941, Karen Horney had led a cohort of her followers out of the New York Psychoanalytic Institute literally singing, "Let My People Go!" But unlike Fromm and Horney, Kohut was no dissident. Indeed, he served as the president of the American Psychoanalytic Association, the bastion of classical Freudian analysis in the United States. In those years he thought of himself as "Mr. Psychoanalysis." But his paper "Introspection, Empathy, and Psychoanalysis" was the first step in what would become a thoroughgoing challenge to the Freudian world-view.

Freud's vision was that psychoanalysis would become a true science of the mind. And for Freud, science was synonymous with objectivity. In Kohut's words, Freud "gazed at man's inner life with the objectivity of an external observer, i.e., from the viewpoint that the scientist of his day had perfected vis-à-vis man's external surroundings, in the biological sciences and, above all, in physics. The

adoption of this basic stance had a profound influence on the for-
mation of the theoretical framework of psychoanalysis."

From a Buddhist perspective, this meant Freud bequeathed to
psychoanalytic theory a profoundly dualistic way of thinking about
mind, body, and the way in which we know the world. Freud's ideal
scientist-observer was separate, neutral, and objective, one whose
influence on the object of observation could be either discounted or
itself carefully observed and subtracted from the equation. Kohut's
first challenge to this stance was to assert that the mode of observation in psychoanalysis was fundamentally different from that
employed by the biological and physical sciences. Introspection and
empathy—the analyst's imaginative immersion in the subjective
experience of another—were irreducible to any quantifiable or
objective scientific mode of observation. Though unremarked by
Kohut at the time, this distinction between the modes of observation of the natural sciences and the human sciences echoes a principle first enunciated by Giovanni Vico in *Scienza Nuova* in 1725.
Isaiah Berlin's summary of Vico's insight could equally describe
Kohut's emphasis on the centrality of introspection and empathy:

> Men's knowledge of the external world which we
> can observe, describe, classify, reflect upon, and of
> which we can record the regularities in time and
> space, differs in principle from their knowledge of
> the world that they themselves create, and which
> obeys rules that they have themselves imposed on
> their creations...of which they therefore have an
> "inside" view.... [T]he story of effort, struggle, pur-
> poses, motives, hopes, fears, attitudes, can therefore
> be known in this superior—"inside"—fashion, for
> which our knowledge of the external world cannot
> possibly be the paradigm—a matter about which the

Cartesians, for whom natural knowledge is the model, must therefore be in error.

With empathy, one ceased to be a separate, objective observer. The analyst's task now became to see the world through the patient's eyes, and to immerse himself in the internal logic of that point of view. Furthermore, empathic immersion is not simply a new mode of data gathering. Empathy itself, Kohut claimed, "is a therapeutic action in the broadest sense, a beneficial action in the broadest sense of the word." In other words, empathy as a mode of observation is inextricably intertwined with empathy as a therapeutic agent in its own right. Our empathic inquiry results both in our better understanding of our patient and in our patient's *feeling understood*. Thus, the inquiry itself transforms the subjective state it inquires into. No impartial, neutral, or scientifically objective inquiry is, in principle, separable from the transformative, therapeutic nature of the inquiry itself.

Kohut did not stop at reconceptualizing the nature of psychoanalytic investigation; he went on to challenge Freud's classic division of the mind into the id, ego, and superego. Freud's model of the mind was organized around the notion of intra-psychic conflict—an eternal, biologically determined war between the irrational drives of the id for sex and aggression, the demands of reality (the ego), and the threats of a punitive conscience (the superego). Kohut, on the other hand, focused on personal, subjective experiences of our *self:* all the conscious and unconscious qualities that constituted our individual sense of identity, personal continuity, meaning, and meaningful relationship.

Kohut's challenge to the Freudian model grew out of his own treatment of patients suffering from what are called narcissistic personality disorders. This diagnosis can include a broad range of symptoms but is focused on disruptions in self-esteem and the inability to sustain a positive, stable sense of one's identity. These patients would typically suffer from a fragile sense of their self-worth or experience extreme volatility in their self-esteem, and are therefore vulnerable to intense mood-swings in the face of praise or criticism. Often hypochondriacal complaints, sexual problems, or addictions develop as their body image, or their sense of physical integrity, undergoes disruptions paralleling the disruptions to their mental self-image. Additionally, pervasive feelings of empty depression or damage may underlie the patient's brittle grandiose façade.

What struck Kohut about these patients was that their symptoms could not easily be explained using a model of intra-psychic conflict. In particular, they did not seem to develop the classic Oedipal transferences, centered around erotic longings or competitive rivalries focused on the analyst along with the corresponding fear of retaliation in the form of castration anxiety, that Freudian theory led one to expect—and at this stage Kohut was still a good Freudian. As a consequence, these patients did not do well in traditional analyses, and were often considered unanalyzable. But, Kohut discovered, once one was willing to broaden the definition of transference beyond Freud's original formulation, one could see that these patients developed their own unique transference configurations—which Kohut dubbed the *narcissistic* transferences. These transferences, rather than making the analyst into the object of sexual or aggressive fantasies, were primarily concerned with longings for attention, particularly the attention of idealized parental figures. (We might think of them literally as attention-deficit disorders!)

Kohut's model for therapy was essentially *developmental*: early failures in parental responsiveness gave rise to a fragile sense of self, and that fragile self needed the experience of a new, emotionally nutritive environment within the analysis to proceed with its growth. But this should not be construed to mean that Kohut advocated a merely supportive, emotionally corrective experience. What he found these patients most lacked was feeling understood, and this included the analyst's providing interpretations that allowed the patient to put their experience into a meaningful context and that explained how and why their emotional reactions had come to be shaped as they were. Because of the fragility of these patients' sense of self and their propensity to feeling misunderstood, much of the interpretative work revolved around identifying and repairing disruptions in the therapeutic relationship precipitated by the analyst's almost inevitable failure to stay perfectly attuned to the patient's subjective state.

When I started my psychiatric training in 1975, Kohut's ideas were still new and had not penetrated into my program's curriculum. It was only after the publication of his second book, *The Restoration of the Self,* in 1977 that I gradually became aware of his ideas. But even though I wasn't sure how to choose between all the different flavors of analysis that one could sample in New York City, I knew I wanted to begin psychoanalytic training someday, so I began looking around for an analyst with whom I could start treatment. Psychiatry in those days wasn't as completely devoted to psychopharmacology as it is today, and a number of psychoanalysts from a variety of Freudian and non-Freudian traditions were members of my hospital's staff. Following their suggestions, I arranged to have an initial interview with a prominent neo-Freudian analyst who, as it happened, was the coauthor of the textbook that we were studying on how to conduct an initial interview. I met with this eminent figure in his hospital office, and he arrived for our appointment wearing a long white lab coat. He sat down behind a large desk, took out a yellow legal pad, and began asking me all the standard questions that he had outlined in his book about my symptoms and my personal history. I felt that the process was about as personal as if I had come in complaining of lower abdominal pain. After about twenty-five minutes of this, I got up and walked out on him.

(For one hoping for an eventual job in our teaching hospital, this was not a good career move.) No doubt, he drew a line across the bottom of his yellow pad and scrawled "unanalyzable."

This style of initial interview was intended not only to gather information but to test a candidate's level of frustration tolerance. Would I be able to lie on the couch while a mostly silent, non-responsive analyst took notes on my free associations? Clearly, in my case, his conclusion would have been no, I couldn't handle it. I was one of those unanalyzable narcissistic personalities—or worse, a *borderline* personality disorder, someone who responded to frustration with impulsive, aggressive behavior (like slamming the door on a famous psychoanalyst). I eventually found a good fit with another analyst who conducted his initial interview in a thoroughly unortho-dox manner. He gave me a big, welcoming smile, and listened intently as I rattled on about my opinion of an article in the *New York Review of Books* that I had just read in his waiting room.

When given this kind of emotional space in which to grow, the transferences that (we) narcissistic patients develop allow us to grad-ually use the attention of the empathically attuned analyst to strengthen our sense of self. Kohut called this experience and use of the analyst a *selfobject* transference. In the classically understood Oedipal transference, the analyst is unconsciously made the *object* of erotic and aggressive wishes. A selfobject is a person experienced in such a way that fosters the cohesion and stability of the patient's self. Kohut eventually came to believe that everyone had selfobject needs of one variety or another and that these were not confined to those suffering from any particular disorder. Even Freud's Oedipal complex would eventually be reconceptualized in terms of the par-ents' failure to respond phase-appropriately to the child's newly emergent sexual and competitive feelings.

Selfobject experiences can take a variety of forms, of which Kohut distinguished three broad types: mirroring, twinship, and idealizing. In a mirroring selfobject transference, the patient longs˙ for an analyst who is perfectly accepting and appreciative of the patient's sense of their own hitherto neglected specialness; in twin-ship, the patient fantasizes an analyst who thinks, feels, and relates in ways identical to the patient; and in an idealizing transference, the patient feels sustained or enlivened by the connection to what is felt to be the analyst's strength, calmness, or power.

We can also broadly distinguish *archaic* from *mature* forms of selfobject experience. Archaic selfobject experiences, which emerge in narcissistic transferences, are characterized by their extreme fragility and specificity. Unless the analyst's attunement and respon-siveness is just so, the experience collapses. What or who can be experienced as a selfobject is unconsciously very narrowly defined and easily missed or spoiled.

It's very much like what happens when my wife and I put our two-year-old son Sam to sleep at night. We have to go through an elaborate, highly specific ritual of bathing, tooth-brushing, and story-reading. When we do all of these things in just the right way, at just the right pace, Sam goes off to bed quietly. But if we are tired or try to rush things, he immediately picks up on our less-than-total interest or our less-than-perfect timing, and the soothing qual-ity of the ritual is disrupted. Sam's need for a highly specific bedtime ritual is completely normal for his age, as is his expectation that we, as his parents, should be attuned to his needs and not let our own intrude. To expect him to be "reasonable" about inevitable or inad-vertent disruptions to his routine would be asking him not to behave like the two-year-old that he is.

Kohut suggested that the selfobject transference demands of some patients needed to be viewed in the same way. A therapeutic approach that tried to interpret to the patient how irrational, dis-torted, self-defeating, or inappropriate those expectations were would only cause further frustration and disruption. While the analyst is not in a position to literally gratify or comply with a patient's every wish, he is in a position to understand and acknowledge the subjective validity of those wishes. Often a willingness simply to see things from the patient's point of view, without comment or attempts at corrective "reality testing," enables the longed-for self-object connection to coalesce.

Although this may sound simple, it is a stance that many therapists and analysts find deeply counterintuitive. Much of our earlier training may have led us to expect that it is precisely our job to discover what is dysfunctional or unrealistic about our patients' ways of thinking and behaving. Interpretations are devised to point out these misperceptions and self-defeating strategies, or even to help the patient devise new modes of behavior more likely to serve his needs. Sometimes when I'm asked to explain what I think is unique about self psychology, I say that it is the one technique that doesn't help anybody! Instead, self psychology presumes that a fragile self will spontaneously grow stronger and more cohesive in an empathically attuned selfobject relationship. That stronger self can be trusted to be essentially self-righting. Back on its developmental track, the self is able to partake of an ever broader range of experience and organize that experience in progressively more satisfying ways.

As this development progresses, a broader range of responses and experiences are utilized as *mature* selfobjects. This progression from *specificity* to *nonspecificity* of selfobject experience is one of the single most reliable hallmarks of emotional maturation. In part, we can say this comes about because one is gradually building up an internal system of values and ideals (through identification with, and internalization of, idealized aspects of the analyst or other parental or mentoring figures) that allows one meaningfully to engage an ever broader range of experience. In its simplest and most mundane form, we don't have to be treated "just so" by our spouses or friends or coworkers in order to feel loved, understood, or respected. At the apex of maturity, we might recall the example of Socrates, as recounted in Plato's *Apology,* who claims that a good man cannot be harmed—even as he is being put on trial for his life. Socrates is a philosopher, and he has reached a stage at which everything, even his own impending death, is an opportunity to philosophize and teach. Every situation in which he finds himself, even the most extreme or traumatic, offers him the opportunity for meaningful engagement and reaffirmation of who he is.

Note that *selfobject* is not hyphenated; the self of the patient and that of the analyst seemingly are merged into one entity. For Kohut, a person's sense of self never exists in isolation; the self is actually the *combination* or *interaction* of the individual self, as traditionally conceived, with its world of selfobjects. Even our subjective experience of *will*, that capacity to initiate or choose a particular course of action, which traditionally has been one of the hallmarks of an individual "self," may be particularly sensitive to or dependent on the selfobject milieu. With the concept of the selfobject, Kohut transformed the psychoanalytic picture of the separate, autonomous self into a contextualized, interdependent self, a self much closer to the picture of dependent co-origination that we find in Buddhism: not only is everything part of an interconnected whole, but each "thing" has no fixed or separate identity apart from its myriad, mutually causal relationships. This idea would be carried even further in the work of the intersubjectivity theorists Robert Stolorow and George Atwood, who, as we shall see in chapter 7, explicitly attack what they call the "myth of the isolated mind."

In 1984, Stolorow coauthored with Bernard Brandchaft a paper provocatively titled "The Borderline Concept: Pathological Character or Iatrogenic Myth?" The 1994 edition of the standard psychiatric diagnostic manual, *DSM-IV*, characterizes the borderline personality disorder as a distinct pathological entity whose features include "a pervasive pattern of instability of interpersonal relationships, self-image, and affect, and marked impulsivity beginning by early childhood," along with a variety of other diagnostic criteria. Brandchaft and Stolorow radically proposed, however, that there was no such thing as a borderline *character*. Rather, the instabilities noted by the *DSM* emerged only in specific contexts—particularly in contexts of therapy that denied the impact of the analyst's mode of inquiry on the patient's experience and that insisted on locating the problem exclusively inside the individual. The so-called syndrome was, in fact, an artifact of an unempathic, medical model of treatment—like my initial interview with that eminent analyst—an iatrogenic (i.e., caused by the doctor) chimera. Borderline patients were actually indistinguishable from Kohut's narcissistic patients when they were responded to in a way that allowed the needed selfobject connection to emerge. What had been described medically as a pathological condition in an individual was actually a by-product of the disruption or lack of attunement on the part of the patient's selfobject milieu. Stolorow and Brandchaft would go on to assert that "the intersubjective context has a constitutive role in *all* forms of psychopathology."

In summary, then, Heinz Kohut's self psychology, amplified by the later contributions of intersubjectivity, transformed Freud's view of the mind in ways that opened up new possibilities for a conceptual rapprochement with Buddhism. These included:

1. Replacing a dualistic observational stance that presumed the possibility of an independent, objective observer with an empathic observer who enters into the world of the observed.

2. Acknowledging the impossibility of pure objectivity or neutrality and the inevitable impact of any mode of observation.

3. Reconceptualizing the structure of the mind in terms of a "self" that organizes experience around a person's own subjectively

defined needs for attention, value, meaning, ambitions, ideals, self-esteem, and emotional attachment rather than around the regulation of universal, biological predetermined drives, fantasies, and intra-psychic conflicts.

4. Recognizing that the "self" does not exist as a separate, fixed entity solely "inside" the person but is constituted relationally within an ever-changing selfobject or intersubjective field.

CHAPTER TWO

TOP-DOWN
PRACTICE: MU

Having set the stage for our ongoing dialogue between Zen and psychoanalysis by providing an introduction to Heinz Kohut's self psychology and Stolorow, Atwood, and Brandchaft's intersubjectivity theory, let me now say something about what one does when one practices Zen. As is the case with psychoanalysis, there are many schools of Buddhism, and within Zen Buddhism there are many traditions and styles, in part corresponding to whether that style originated in China, Korea, Japan, or Vietnam. My own experience has been with different branches of Japanese Zen. For our purposes, all these various practices can be roughly divided into two basic types, which I like to call top-down and bottom-up.

In this chapter, I will focus on "top-down" practice, and outline what I believe are both its powers and its pitfalls. In the next chapter, I will contrast it with the "bottom-up" practice that I myself practice and teach. A top-down practice is a concentration practice, such as working on the koan *Mu*. In contrast to the sort of practice where one simply watches thoughts come and go, with Mu one attempts to keep all of one's attention focused on the koan as continuously and as intently as possible. Traditionally, this is the first koan assigned in Rinzai Zen temples, and it was the focus of my own practice during the years I was in training to be a psychiatrist and psychoanalyst. The word *koan* means "public case," and back then I liked to think of koans as the Zen equivalent of the famous clinical cases we studied, like Freud's Rat Man and Wolf Man. A koan attempts to encapsulate a psychological or philosophical conundrum in the form of a simple story, dialogue, or riddle, usually within the context of a dramatic encounter between an old master and one of his students. But unlike psychological case studies, these encounters are not meant to be studied or discussed so much as reenacted. Each student poses these crucial questions anew for himself and must reach his own immediate experience of their solution.

Practicing with Mu has its origin in the story of a famous encounter between a student and the Chinese Zen master Chao-chou. The monk asked Chao-chou, "Does a dog have the Buddha nature?" Chao-chou's answer, "Mu," literally means "no," even though it is one of the most basic tenets of the historical Buddha's original teaching that every sentient being possesses Buddha nature. Generations of Zen students have been challenged to present to their teachers the meaning of Chao-chou's "Mu." One practices with this first koan by concentrating all one's attention on silently repeating the single syllable *Mu*, breath after breath after breath. Everything becomes this one sound *Mu*. I breathe *Mu* in and out; *Mu* breathes me in and out. Outside and inside disappear, the boundaries between the self and the world disappear, and there is only *this*. When we are nothing but *this*, there is no separation: no separate self, no separate object of experience. No "has" or "has not" Buddha nature.

But as a psychoanalyst in training, I kept wondering what kind of insight this could be. Insights, in the Freudian tradition at least, always involved making the unconscious conscious: a hitherto repressed childhood sexual or aggressive wish was at long last remembered and acknowledged. One's mind was then no longer in constant conflict with itself, and life could go on unburdened by the guilt or anxiety that those forbidden wishes had unconsciously engendered. My own (non-Freudian) analysis never unearthed any repressed memories or traumas. Rather, it seemed to me a process of slowly coming to understand the way that my parents' own anxieties had had an impact on my childhood, setting up fearful boundaries within me as to who and what I might become and what I might expect from the world. I realized how much I longed for idealizable mentors, people whose lives were not as constricted as those of my parents, and who would embody freedom, possibility, and vitality. Both my analyst and my Zen teacher seemed to fit the bill, but they had apparently gotten there by two very different routes. What did it imply for psychoanalytic theory if Zen teachers could achieve freedom seemingly without reaching any insight into their early childhood, family relations, and unconscious wishes—the *sine qua non* of change for my analytic mentors?

Whatever kind of insight Mu offered was obviously of a qualitatively different kind altogether from what I was used to calling an insight in my psychoanalytic vocabulary. Yet, I had already had some intimations of that different kind of insight. While I was a medical student taking my first course in psychiatry, I sat in on a large group therapy session of patients, therapists, and other students. Looking around the room, I suddenly was filled with the realization that everyone in the room was being themselves *perfectly*. No matter who they were or what their problems seemed to have been just a moment before, suddenly everyone was just who they were, doing what they did. How could they make a mistake at that? Though the joy of that moment was short-lived, it somehow carried itself forward in a subtly altered way of looking at things that I could not explain.

Further along in my psychoanalytic training, while I was still working on Mu, I had an unusual dream: Walking along a familiar street, I suddenly came upon my own dead body in the gutter. Astonished, I bent down to see if that's what it really was. As I did so, a black-robed figure appeared and asked me my name. "Barry Magid," I answered. Pointing to the corpse, the figure again asked my name, and again I answered, "Barry Magid." A third time, the figure pointed to the dead body and again asked my name. This time I could only reply, "I don't know." Then the figure said, "You can have anything you want." I was dumbstruck and didn't know what to ask for, when I noticed he was now holding a can of soda. I pointed to that and asked for a sip, which he gave me. I then walked away, dazzled by the sunlight on the street.

Even taken out of its original context, I think we can see how this dream might portend the sudden dissolution of an old sense of who I was, the "death" of an old identity, and the emergence of a new, more open sense of self and possibility. But what brought it about? And what relationship did the dream's message have to the interpretations I was used to hearing from my analyst? In the case of this particular dream, I remember, my analyst offered no interpretation at all—except for a big smile.

I called working with Mu a top-down practice because it is intended to induce a peak experience of oneness. In traditional Zen terminology, we would speak of encountering the absolute, as opposed to our ordinary, relative world of dualism and differentiation. This way of practicing presumes that each time we have an experience of the absolute, the self we return to is subtly transformed, its boundaries less rigid and defended. It is as if something trickles down from that mystical peak to permanently alter who we are down below in our day-to-day life.

This type of practice inevitably raises questions: How exactly are we supposed to bring that peak experience of nonseparation or oneness down into our everyday life? Is it something that happens spontaneously or something we need to practice? Should the focus of our practice always be the goal of repeating such experiences as deeply and as often as possible, or is there another step to take? At this point, a traditional Zen master might challenge his student to show how he can "take a step off the top of a hundred-foot pole." But who would want to take such a step? Don't we all imagine that it would be better to remain in some lofty, mystical state than to return to our everyday lives?

Meditators face a very real danger of coming to prefer the view from the top of the pole to their real life on the ground. But such peak moments, no matter how profound, always end, leaving us with the problem of how to live in accord with the perspective they provide. Unless we learn how to step off the pole, our practice will devolve into a mere addiction to the highs of peak experience.

CHAO-CHOU'S DOG

The Case

*A monk asked Chao-chou, "Has the dog Buddha nature
    or not?"*
Chao-chou said, "Mu."

Wu-men's Comment

*For the practice of Zen it is imperative that you pass through
the barrier set up by the Ancestral Teachers. For subtle realization it is of utmost importance that you cut off the mind
road. If you do not pass this barrier of the ancestors, if you do
not cut off the mind road, then you are a ghost clinging to
bushes and grasses.*

*What is the barrier of the Ancestral Teachers? It is just this
one word, "Mu"—the one barrier of our faith. We call it the Gateless Barrier of the Zen tradition. When you pass through this barrier, you will not only interview Chao-chou intimately, you will
walk hand-in-hand with all the Ancestral Teachers in the successive generations of our lineage—the hair of your eyebrows entangled with theirs, seeing with the same eyes, hearing with the same
ears. Won't that be fulfilling? Is there anyone who would not want
to pass this barrier?*

*So, then, make your whole body a mass of doubt, and with
your three hundred and sixty bones and joints and your eighty-four
thousand hair follicles concentrate on this one word "Mu." Day
and night, keep digging into it. Don't consider it to be nothingness.
Don't think in terms of "has" and "has not." It is like swallowing a
red-hot iron ball. You try to vomit it out, but you can't.*

Gradually you purify yourself, eliminating mistaken knowledge and attitudes you have held from the past. Inside and outside become one. You're like a mute person who has had a dream—you know it for yourself alone.

Suddenly Mu breaks open. The heavens are astonished, the earth is shaken. It is as if you have snatched the great sword of General Kuan. When you meet the Buddha, you kill the Buddha. When you meet Bodhidharma, you kill Bodhidharma. At the very cliff edge of birth-and-death, you find Great Freedom. In the Six Worlds and the Four Modes of Birth, you enjoy a samadhi of frolic and play.

How, then, should you work with it? Exhaust all your life energy on this one word "Mu." If you do not falter, then it's done! A single spark lights your Dharma candle.

> *Dog, Buddha nature—*
> *The full presentation of the whole;*
> *With a bit of "has" or "has not"*
> *Body is lost, life is lost.*

This is the first of forty-eight cases in the *Wu-men Kuan*, a thirteenth-century collection of koans. Aitken Roshi, whose version I have given here, translates *Wu-men Kuan* as *The Gateless Barrier*. Earlier translators have called it *The Gateless Gate*. We should realize how much of our practice is contained just in that title. What is the title telling us? When we first hear of a gateless barrier, we may imagine that it means an impenetrable barrier, one with no opening or gate anywhere. But actually it means just the opposite: that life is wide-open to us just as it is—that there really is no barrier anywhere. But we don't experience our lives this way at all, do we? We feel that there are barriers everywhere, inside and out—barriers that we don't want to face or cross, barriers of fear, anger, pain, old age, and death. Our practice consists of nothing but learning to recognize these barriers one after another, and then facing them. And when we are really willing to enter the territory they have shut off from us, we find ourselves in that wide-open, barrierless life that Wu-men wanted to help us discover.

At the most basic level then, these old stories, and especially this story about Chao-chou, are all about the problem of separation, about the artificial barriers we experience between ourselves and life as it is. And Wu-men is offering a technique of concentrating on one word, Chao-chou's "Mu," as a way of breaking down these barriers. By trying to become completely absorbed in Mu, the student, then as now, will first bump up against his own barriers, and then, by filling his whole consciousness with Mu, his whole world with Mu, the barriers themselves will disappear along with everything else into this one word. Wu-men summarizes these barriers in the phrase "has or has not" and thinks of them as essentially consisting of our thoughts and concepts.

Today, we are more prepared to see the emotional underpinnings of our barriers. When Wu-men speaks of "great doubt," at one level we can feel the overwhelming confusion and perplexity of the monk trying to reach an intellectual understanding of Chao-chou's truly incomprehensible answer. The monk must come face to face with the deep, seemingly unbridgeable sense of separation that thought incessantly creates (in this case the thought of "Buddha nature," which feels millions of miles away from the real world of dogs and ordinary monks) and that we become acutely aware of as we begin to practice. The "red-hot iron ball" that we can neither swallow nor spit up is a picture of how it feels to come to grips with that painful sense of separation we don't know how to escape. But paradoxically, "great doubt" is also the way we eliminate that gap—

because in the midst of doubt and not knowing, our habitual ways of thinking and separating ourselves from the world lose their grip. We truly become Mu only when we have finally ceased to understand it.

Today, we practice by focusing on our own inner barriers, one by one, especially the emotional barriers of fear, pain, emptiness, and anger that manifest as hard knots of bodily tension. These are truly red-hot iron balls. These are feelings we've tried to stay separate from, and to keep them at bay we have erected barriers between ourselves and life. I've often said that analysis, paradoxically, is a process in which we must come to *distrust* our deepest feelings—to question all that we are so sure is at stake when we keep parts of ourselves and our life at bay.

Wu-men asks, What is Mu? This is precisely like asking, "What is life?" And you can't answer by somehow standing outside of life, examining it, and offering your description. You yourself must become the answer.

CHAPTER THREE

BOTTOM-UP PRACTICE: JUST SITTING

A BOTTOM-UP PRACTICE proceeds in the opposite direction to the top-down practice of koan study. This practice is sometimes called "just sitting" and is characteristic of the Soto Zen school. Here the premise is that zazen is already the perfect manifestation of the awakened way. We don't sit in order to *become* Buddhas; we sit because we already *are* Buddhas. Now, the fact is that most of the time we don't feel much like Buddhas—or rather, we can't believe that *this* is what it feels like to be Buddha. So any practice of "just sitting" immediately runs into this sense of resistance. And rather than attempting to induce experiences of oneness, we practice staying with the resistance itself. The two basic hallmarks of resistance in our lives are fear and anger. These emotions mark off what we don't want to accept or face, where the self feels it is not getting its way or not being treated the way it wants.

It's at this level that Zen and psychotherapy practices dovetail. I am aware of no psychoanalytic equivalent to a top-down concentration practice specifically designed to induce experiences of "oneness." But a bottom-up practice of just sitting that focuses attention on resistance, on emotional and bodily tension, leads to questions familiar to every analyst and analysand: "Who do I think I am?

What do I think I need to change about myself? What do I feel capable of? What feels impossible or crazy? What do I expect from others? What must I avoid at all costs?" Taken together, our answers to these sorts of questions may be called our *core beliefs:* our personal, conditioned view of the world, which masquerades in our life as "common sense." Uncovering and making explicit the arbitrary nature of our core beliefs is the common goal of Zen and all psychoanalytically oriented psychotherapy.

In this practice of just sitting, the student begins sitting with a simple focus on the sensation of breathing in and out. As thoughts come and go, we label them simply as "thought" and return our attention to our breath. (One good technique for labeling thoughts is simply to silently say to oneself, "thinking...such and such," and repeating the thought to yourself. If this gets too wordy, we might use a simple phrase like "worrying" as a label for a recurrent pattern of thought.) Gradually we learn to settle into the silence behind our thoughts. In that silence we simply experience the physicality of sitting. As we sit, we become attuned to the physical manifestations of fear and anger in our bodies. These will always be experienced as bodily tension somewhere or another; they are the physical correlates of our psychological guardedness.

When we sit, we bring the focus of our attention right to the boundaries of our experience of separation, right to the physical pain or tension that marks the line we don't want to cross. And that's where we sit, right on that line, right in the midst of that tension. Whatever boundaries the self habitually tries to set up in life, it will try to set up here and now in the zendo: boundaries of judgment of oneself and others, boundaries of how we think we're doing well or badly in our practice, boundaries of expectation regarding other students or the teacher. Whenever our fear or anger illuminates one of these boundaries, that's where we put down our cushion. In this way of practicing, oneness is experienced as an all-inclusive "being just this moment."

JUST SITTING

Although we speak in simple terms of "just sitting" and of cultivating an awareness of our resistance to "being just this moment" by labeling our thoughts and experiencing the tension in our bodies, if we go back to Dogen and look at the text of his famous talk, "Recommending Zazen to All People," delivered in the year 1227, what we read there may not appear quite so simple and straightforward as I've described it. After describing the correct posture for zazen, Dogen says, "Now sit steadfastly and think not-thinking. How do you think not-thinking? Beyond thinking. This is the essential art of zazen."

What does Dogen mean by "think not-thinking"? I'm afraid "beyond thinking" doesn't clarify things much for most of us, so let me try to go into this in some detail. First of all, he doesn't say, "Don't think." He's not saying we must try to have a completely blank mind. But obviously he is also not saying, "Just go ahead and daydream" either. Notice too that he isn't suggesting that we practice any simple repetitive concentration practice like focusing on Mu, repeating a mantra, or counting breaths. "Think not-thinking" must mean something else entirely.

Our usual way of thinking is to think *about* something—we sit and think about something *out there* that our thoughts are describing or imagining. This kind of thinking is characterized by its descriptive content—what it's *about*. But what if instead of focusing on the content of thought, we see thought as an activity in its own right? As something that we, or our body, *does*? Our foot itches, our knee hurts, our head thinks. It is just this perspective that labeling our thoughts brings about. When we repeat the thought "thinking about 'the cat on the mat,'" our attention is no longer on the cat but on ourselves having a thought, engaging in the activity of thinking. Often in Zen literature we find the words *not-doing* used to refer to a not-separate mode of functioning. No thinker having a thought. Just the activity of thinking. And what Dogen means here by "think not-thinking" is that not-separate activity of thinking—a thinking that is just the activity of thinking itself, as he says, beyond thinking *about* anything.

What was Dogen's attitude to koans? It's hard to say. He did compile a collection of koans for study and commentary, but scholars and teachers differ on how it would have been used. John Daido Loori Roshi, a lineage holder in both the Rinzai and Soto traditions, maintains he is simply following Dogen's own practice in using the cases in Dogen's *Chinese Shobogenzo* as part of his own students' traditional koan practice. But the scholar T. Griffith Foulk claims that in "medieval Japanese monasteries associated with the Soto lineage, koans were widely used in the contexts of public sermons and private meetings between master and disciples, but koan commentary was not linked with seated meditation in the manner of the 'Zen of contemplating phrases.'" In other words, monks were not instructed to concentrate on a word like *Mu* or some other phrase from a koan during zazen—though they might be spontaneously challenged to show their understanding of a koan during an interview with the teacher. However they were used, many modern scholars agree that Dogen would have rejected any "instrumentalist" use of koans merely as a means for inducing kensho. Rather, what is depicted in the koan is, in Dogen's phrase, the ongoing "actualization of enlightenment" (*genjokoan*). I cannot venture an opinion on the historical question of Dogen's actual practice, but for me koans offer a view of nonduality in action, and challenge us to see the world through the clear eyes of the old masters. I offer my own commentaries in that spirit. But I do subscribe to the traditional Soto separation of koan commentary from sitting practice, in that I generally do not ask my students to concentrate on koans like Mu while sitting. We need to work instead on our natural koans: the residues of separation in our own lives and in our own core beliefs, manifesting in the tensions and resistances that appear in our bodies as we sit.

Although at one level, we can distinguish the schools of Zen in terms of different meditative techniques, fundamentally zazen is not a technique at all. A technique is something to master, something you can do well or badly. But when it comes to sitting, the truth is we can't do it wrong. Whatever we experience, whatever doubt or difficulty we face, is simply who and what we are in that moment. To experience the moment as it occurs is to be the Buddha of that moment. All our techniques are nothing but reminders of this simple fact. As we read in the *Sandokai:* "If you do not see the Way, you do not see it even as you walk on it." Over time, our trust in sitting deepens and we see what's been there all along.

After years of mature practice, the distinction between the two directions, top-down versus bottom-up, dissolves. Ultimately, both lead to simply being present and responsive to each moment as it is, including an awareness of our thoughts and emotional resistances as just momentary phenomena that we experience as they pass.

THE GOOSE IN THE BOTTLE

An old koan asks, "How can you get a goose out of a bottle?"

Imagine that a baby gosling was placed inside one of those big glass bottles with small mouths that you see model ships in; the goose is now full grown and cannot fit through the neck of the bottle. How can you get it out? It's frightening to imagine what an artificial and constricted life that poor goose must have led. In such conditions, how unimaginable a life of freedom must be. And yet, that's what the old teacher who thought up this koan was saying about our lives—that we lead lives so confined and constricted that we can hardly begin to imagine what true freedom is like.

If we're ever going to be free, it is essential that we come to understand the nature of the bottle that constrains us. It's interesting to compare the imagery of this koan with something the philosopher Ludwig Wittgenstein wrote in his *Philosophical Investigations:* the goal of philosophy is to show the fly the way out of the fly-bottle. For Wittgenstein, the fly-bottle was built out of our misunderstandings about how language works in our lives. For example, we imagine we look "inside" and describe inner mental landscapes the same way we look "outside" and describe the world. Or we imagine that nobody but me can see my inner landscape— it's unique and private. When we think this way, we get entangled in misunderstandings about the nature and privacy of so-called inner experience. We think that the "I" is "inside" and that the meaning of words is something that begins inside our heads and needs to somehow be projected "out" onto objects in the world. But Wittgenstein argued that language—and the self—is always interpersonal and contextual, never private. To think that inner experience and the meaning of language (and life) is intrinsically individual, subjective, and private leads to solipsism—turning our skulls into bottles, and our minds into geese!

For Wittgenstein, as for us as both Zen students and analysands, the only way out of the bottle is through the close, careful examination of the bottle itself. Wittgenstein urged us over and over to look at how words are actually *used*. A word's use is always grounded in some human activity. Meaning is never static or definable outside contexts of actual use. We must watch how our words function in our life, and not assume that they are once and for all attached to objects in the world like labels on plants in a botanical garden.

In our practice, how do we understand what constrains our lives?

If we want to describe the bottle in the most general terms, we could say (in the version of the Four Bodhisattva Vows we chant in our zendo at the end of each day's sitting) that we're "caught in a self-centered dream." But each of us needs to be more specific. We need to explore the constriction we find in our own bodies, the tension that holds all the old hurts, and fears, and defenses. We need to see what walls we unconsciously have set up, what lines we are unwilling to cross, what we are afraid to face, what we are trying to shield ourselves from. Some of you who are of a certain age may remember an old toothpaste commercial that promised that its product would put up a "Guard-All" shield between the tooth and the forces of tooth decay. In a way, that is how all our bottles get built in the first place. We try to put up a shield between ourselves and life, thinking to protect ourselves from suffering. And these shields do work in their way, and perhaps at vulnerable times in our lives, we've felt we couldn't live without them. But ultimately they turn from being walls that protect to walls that imprison. One day we wake up and realize that we've crawled into a glass bottle to hide, and now we don't know how to get out.

If we work on this koan in the context of a top-down practice, there may come a day when the bottle suddenly disappears; inside and outside disappear and the goose is free to fly off in any direction. But in the very next moment, our goose is likely to be back inside the bottle. We've had a taste of freedom, but haven't worked through the self-centeredness that constrains our everyday life. If you just treat this koan as a riddle, the answer isn't so difficult—but neither will it make any difference in your life when you solve it. Practicing with it in a bottom-up way means taking the time to thoroughly study the bottle, and not being in any hurry to fly off with the goose.

CHAPTER FOUR

SELF AND ONENESS

PRACTICING WITH MU, we may encounter a peak experience of oneness. In the practice of just sitting, we find less emphasis on peak experiences and more on simply being in the moment, including being aware of our resistance to staying with our moment-by-moment experience. The sort of oneness we find by just sitting seems, on the surface at least, to be of a different kind altogether from that revealed by Mu. How are these versions of oneness related? How do we go from talking about oneness as a unique but transitory subjective experience to understanding how oneness functions in our daily lives? Can a psychoanalytic perspective help us with these questions? More specifically, what do the new psychoanalytic perspectives of self psychology and intersubjectivity have to say about oneness?

Let's begin by looking back at what oneness meant within a Freudian psychoanalytic vocabulary. Ever since Freud referred to a feeling of "limitlessness and of a bond to the universe" as the "oceanic feeling," much psychoanalytic ink has been spilled over this question. Freud was not prepared to follow the example of his American contemporary William James, who treated religious experiences as important psychological data that might significantly shape our picture of human nature and of the self. Locked into a perspective in which scientific objectivity represented the epitome of mental and cultural development, Freud thought that religious experience was perforce illusionary, and only explainable in terms of defensive wishful thinking or a pathological suspension of reality of the sort that occurs in psychotic delusions. This meant, in Freud's view, that any experience of oneness must involve some sort of *regression,* i.e., a return to an earlier or more primitive level of mental functioning. Freud hypothesized that religious experience momentarily returned the meditator or mystic to an infantile developmental level characterized by the sort of loss of differentiation between self and other that is felt by an infant fused to the mother's breast. For years, this theoretical outlook dominated all subsequent psychoanalytic treatment of the subject. Thus, we get explanations of oneness such as this: "Through meditation…a profound but temporary and controlled regression occurs. This deep experience helps the individual regress…to the somato-symbiotic phase of the mother-child relationship." When we decode the jargon, what it comes down to is that when you feel you are at one with the universe, you are actually lost in a fantasy of being back on the tit.

Even when these analysts believed that meditation could be beneficial, they had no conceptual framework other than of regression to explain what was going on. If meditation worked, somehow the sense of childlike well-being evoked by these temporary regressions was supposed to infuse our lives when we returned to "normal."

Is that really what's going on in our practice? Sadly, I run into many meditators who (even if they've never heard of regression) seem to practice just this way. They use meditation to settle into a dreamy, blissful haze and seem to believe that a perpetually sweet, childlike demeanor is the hallmark of true practice. I can't help but smile when I imagine how one of the old Chinese masters would deal with these people! Thirty blows with the stick! But if we don't want to think about, or practice with, oneness in this way, what is the alternative?

The advent of self psychology and intersubjectivity theory offers an entirely new perspective than was possible within the old Freudian model. As we said earlier, one of the main contributions of self psychology was to demonstrate that the adult mind is just as co-determined by its contextual surroundings as that of the infant. The self never exists in isolation but is always constituted within its selfobject milieu. In this way of looking at things, "oneness" suddenly takes on a whole new light. Now, if we talk about a state in which "self and other are neither one, nor two, but somehow together make up an interpenetrating field," it suddenly makes sense as a description of the intersubjective reality that we all, *as adults,* inhabit—not only as a description of the world of the infant, the way it was originally intended.

Psychoanalytic theories that explain religious experience by invoking analogies with a supposedly undifferentiated, symbiotic, or merged infant probably not only misrepresent the baby's subjective experience, but more significantly, look at the wrong end of the developmental spectrum. To nondualistically inhabit reality does not involve regression but constitutes true developmental maturity. Perhaps it's finally time for psychoanalysts to stop thinking that experiencing oneness means momentarily returning to the way things once *were,* and to recognize that it means seeing things as they *are.* Dualism itself constitutes *a developmental failure*, a fundamentally defensive, fantasized attempt to split off the self from a world of potential suffering. In Zen terms, oneness means the absence of dualism's artificial separation between self and world. Zen speaks of this nonseparate self as *no-self:* that is, no *separate* self. When we think of oneness in terms of the ongoing functioning of the nonseparate self, we are not imagining a self devoid of structures and boundaries, like Freud's undifferentiated oceanic state, but rather a self that is fluidly, spontaneously, and meaningfully engaged with life. That engagement utilizes the full panoply of adult values, ideals, and talents. In terms of Kohut's self psychology, we could say that for the no-self, all experiences are mature self-object experiences. That is, the self engages with any and all moment-to-moment experience in a way that directly expresses its values and ideals—or, in traditional Buddhist terms, its wisdom and compassion. It is this *functioning*, not the lapse into some mystical oceanic state, that is the hallmark of the life of oneness.

In the past, most psychoanalytically oriented writers have focused their attention on single, intense moments of revelatory experience—the kind of oneness experiences that Freud could call "the oceanic." Such states do occur in the course of practice, but their import can be very misleading if taken out of the context of how separation or nonseparation actually functions in our day-to-day life. Zen is not concerned with inducing such momentary experiences of oneness for their own sake, but values them (at least potentially) as the instigators of those long-term changes in character and motivation that can accompany the abandonment of a dualistic perspective. If we only focus on those extraordinary moments of experience that are emphasized by a top-down approach to practice, we may be tempted to think of them as unique states that are radically discontinuous from our ordinary consciousness and behavior. Somehow, we hope, their effects will trickle down into our lives.

Being one with our moment-to-moment experience, as we are in the bottom-up practice of just sitting, gives us a taste of nonseparation that is more continuous with our daily lives. Being one with chopping vegetables may sound less glamorous than being one with the universe, but gradually we come to realize the whole universe is contained in that act of chopping. From a theoretical perspective, once we realize that the real goal of practice is nonseparate *functioning* in everyday life, then the whole question of regression becomes irrelevant. Regression, which by definition is a return to some childlike state, precludes our functioning at an adult or mature level. According to this alternative way of thinking about oneness, nondualistic functioning is the expression of our most mature levels of development, in which we continuously and meaningfully engage with a world of which we are all inseparably a part.

Lest you think this is all merely of theoretical interest, let me illustrate some of the themes we've just discussed by way of a parable.

A TALE OF TWO MEDITATORS

Let us imagine two young analysts who have taken up meditation.

Analyst A has been sitting at the local zendo for a few years. One day, while counting his breaths, he gradually feels like he is no longer doing the breathing but is *being breathed*. And then suddenly, he has the sense that he and everyone else are One Body. The world is a living, unified whole. Everything is perfect just as it is.

Though this realization lasts for only a few minutes, when he goes home at the end of the day he is convinced he has had a great mystical experience, the kind he has always hoped to achieve as the result of his sitting. He feels different now, and special. He feels a certain condescension, even pity (which he calls "compassion") for his fellow meditators and analysts who have never had such an experience. Because of his new insight, he is now more convinced than ever of the rightness of his clinical interpretations and begins to believe that his patients partake in some subtle way of his new-found openness and perfection just by being in the same room with him. Convinced of his own essential goodness, he increasingly has trouble imagining that anything he does could have a negative impact on them, and blames their failure to improve on their own entrenched dualism. From now on, when he meditates, he puts all his effort into trying to recapture the feeling of oneness he experienced on that momentous day.

Analyst B has also been meditating for some years but has never had a dramatic experience like the one Analyst A rushed to tell him about. His own sitting, instead of giving him any blissful sense of oneness, has only made him more aware of his own anger and anxiety. He has seen how much he tries to do everything perfectly in the zendo and how frustrated he can get at his limitations. He notices how his shoulders always seem to tense up when he sits rigidly, trying to be the model student and impress his teacher. Gradually he comes to realize that everyone in the zendo is struggling with the same problems and the same pain. Instead of feeling special, he begins to feel more like part of the group, supporting and supported by everything that takes place around him. With his patients, he finds he no longer divides them into two camps—good analyzable prospects and difficult if not impossible borderlines. Now he empathically resonates with a greater range of human suffering; he is more inclined to see everyone who walks through the consulting room door simply as a fellow human being. The differences between himself and his patients no longer seem so profound or relevant. It is not that he has become oblivious to their difficulties, just the opposite. He is more willing to engage with whatever arises in himself and others without pejorative labels or judgments. Differences have stopped making a difference.

In a way, it doesn't matter whether you call Analyst A's experience of oneness "regressive" or not. What does matter is that he immediately incorporated it into his self-centered view of things—his "special" experience confirmed him as a special sort of person. Paradoxically, his realization of "oneness" only increased his sense of his own difference and his separation from everybody around him. Whatever sort of "oneness" this was, it didn't diminish his dualistic thinking in his day-to-day life. Analyst B, on the other hand, progressively became aware of the barriers he had habitually set up between himself and others, and as a result, these barriers gradually and undramatically began to come down. He never had a "mystical" experience, and his life, on the surface, wasn't so different from that of his colleagues who never meditated. But he began to function less and less from a self-centered, dualistic perspective.

NO SEPARATION

When we think of oneness as a kind of peak experience, we have in mind those rare breakthrough moments when all boundaries dissolve and we feel a oneness with the whole universe. But when we look at the functioning of oneness in day-to-day life, we're not talking about walking around in some kind of permanent mystical haze. Rather, we are referring to a capacity to function without separation from whatever we're doing in the moment. *No separation* means acting without holding on to any conceptual picture of oneself as the one acting, or of the object as something acted upon. It's what we mean by *just* doing something. Traditionally, Zen teachers would say that there is no self and no object, and that the separation of the action into subject and object is dissolved in the moment's activity. Just how, from a psychoanalytic perspective, we should understand what aspects of self are lost in such moments, and what must remain in order for us to function at all, is a question that we will address in more detail in subsequent chapters.

One way that the peak experience of oneness comes down to earth is when we unite ourselves with the activities of everyday life. Just doing the dishes, just taking out the trash. After passing the initial koan Mu, a student in traditional Rinzai training may move quickly through a series of koans meant to consolidate the experience by working with the imagery of other koans. Typically, some distant, separate object is designated: perhaps a bell in a far-off temple, or one of two sisters in a room. The teacher might ask, "How do you stop that bell from ringing?" Or "Is that girl the older or younger of the two sisters?" One "answers" such koans by becoming what they are about; one dissolves the apparent separation by enacting the content of the koan. (An aptitude for charades comes in handy at this point!) What really matters, of course, is not one's acting ability but one's capacity to simply throw oneself wholeheartedly into the moment, however arbitrary or absurd that might seem to our ordinary way of thinking.

In Soto practice, where just sitting rather than koan study is the focus of practice, ritual traditionally served as the vehicle for practicing nonseparation in daily life. Putting on a robe, making bows, chanting, and cleaning the toilet all become opportunities for wholehearted participation in the moment. Although the level of attention to detail in a traditional Japanese monastery might strike us as incredibly arbitrary, if not downright obsessive, an unselfconscious and unreserved immersion in particulars becomes the mode of actualization of nonseparation in everyday life. In our daily practice, the hallmark of nonseparation is *no resistance*—the willingness simply to do whatever is next. Styles of Zen diverge at this point; some emphasize the *just doing* over and over as means to gradually erode our resistance. A more psychologically minded practice nowadays also emphasizes an awareness of the individual nature and dynamics of our resistances as well. So, for instance, when anger or some other form of resistance emerges, we try to specify just what expectation or sense of entitlement is being challenged, and to become as clear as possible about just where and when that expectation first arose.

Another koan asks, "Why can't the person of great strength lift up a leg?" Here the riddle of nonseparation is posed in terms of the duality of mind and body. For one thing to act on another, they must be two separate things in the first place. The person of great strength (that is, great spiritual strength and realization) knows no separation, and thus doesn't do anything *to* or *with* his body or his strength; he simply moves and functions. Strength, understood in its broadest sense, stands for the sum of one's unselfconscious and unselfcentered capacities. Today, we would be tempted to parse these into separate categories of innate talents, acquired skills, preconscious values and ideals, and unconscious organizing principles. Much of what appears as spontaneous or natural action in such traditional Japanese disciplines as calligraphy, pottery, or the martial arts is the result of an intensive discipline and training that makes the activity not just second nature but, for all intents and purposes, nature. Reduced to a riddle, this koan is easy to understand; as a challenge to live an unselfconscious, unalienated life, it is one we work on forever.

What would *consistently* functioning from oneness look like? One characteristic of a life lived from a thoroughly nondualistic perspective is that *we no longer have any problems*. That is, we no longer divide our life into the good parts and the problematic parts; there is simply *life*, one moment after another. Problems don't disappear *from* our life, they disappear *into* our life. There needn't be anything particularly special or mystical about it. When we think of oneness in this way, as a nondualistic way of functioning, it is clearly not dependent on any regressive analogue; nor through such functioning are we returned to such a state. Had Analyst A's experience taken place in a different practice context, it might have served to challenge, rather than confirm, his self-centeredness. How we classify any given momentary experience is not crucial. How it functions in our life is what counts.

SUNG-YÜAN'S PERSON
OF GREAT STRENGTH

The Case

*The priest Sung-yüan asked, "Why can't the person of great
strength lift up a leg?"*

Again he said, "It is not with the tongue that you speak."

Wu-men's Comment

*Sung-yüan certainly emptied his stomach and turned out his guts.
However, there is no one who can acknowledge him. Yet even if
someone could immediately acknowledge him, I would give him
a painful blow with my stick if he came to me. Why? Look! If you
want to know true gold, you must perceive it in the midst of fire.*

> *Lifting my leg, I kick the Scented Ocean upside down;*
> *inclining my head, I look down on the four*
> > *Dhyana Heavens;*
> *there is no place to put my complete body—*
> *please add the final line here.*

We ordinarily take for granted our ability to move our bodies,
though in the midst of zazen, when our knees and ankles may be
quite painful, lifting up a leg may not seem such a trivial matter. But
this koan is not concerned with that sort of difficulty; it asks us to
look at the ways we think or feel ourselves separate from our own

bodies. The person of great spiritual strength is someone for whom there is no such separation. He is not separate from his leg, his leg is not an object to him, and so there is no "he" lifting "it."

Wittgenstein applied a very similar argument to pain. He said that we cannot properly say that we "know" that we're in pain because knowing involves a separation into a knower and an object of knowledge. What can be known can also be doubted. I can wonder whether you are in pain or just faking it, but I can't have the same kind of doubt about my own pain. We cannot doubt whether or not we are in pain, and so we cannot know it either. Our words (or screams!) are an *expression* of pain from the midst of being in pain, and are themselves part of what it means to be in pain. R.H. Blyth makes much the same point in his little essay "Zen and Grammar." Blyth warns us even to watch out for the word *express* itself, which he says is "one of the most useful and misleading words in any language. A thing does not express even itself; it just is itself. So…'Blast it!' does not express a feeling of impotent anger. It is part, a potent part, of the impotence of the anger. Without the exclamation there is no anger; without the anger there is no (real) exclamation."

We are not separate disinterested observers of our own experience, somehow standing outside ourselves, looking in and then reporting what we see. We can adopt that way of *talking about* ourselves, but then that way of using language obscures something fundamental about our relationship to our own experience.

Wu-men drives home the point by saying that he would give a painful blow of his stick to anyone who steps forward claiming to know the answer to Sung-yüan's question. But the psychological reality is that most of us experience some degree of alienation from our bodies. We are in the grip of ideas about how they should look and how they should function. We treat our bodies as objects and possessions, being proud or ashamed of their condition or status. All these preconceptions objectify our bodies and so we end up being able to lift our legs—appendages we perceive as strong or weak, muscular or flabby, tanned or pale—precisely because we've turned them into objects separate from ourselves.

Sung-yüan also says, "It is not with the tongue that you speak." Zen is usually portrayed as a practice that goes beyond words, but here the master reminds us that speech is for humans as natural as song is for birds, and we must not alienate ourselves from any of our natural capacities. Words and ideas have their natural use and function, but again, we can all too easily become self-consciously bogged down in images and expectations, and thereby create an artificial gap between our selves and how we express ourselves. Sung-yüan is said to have tested his students with a third question, "Why has the man of great satori not cut the red thread?" The red thread is the thread of passion, of emotion. Do you expect enlightenment (satori) to cut off all passions? Once again, the reminder is that we must be intimate with our emotional life and not use practice to pursue some fantasy of "stone Buddha" detachment, as if becoming insensate were our goal. Taken together, Sung-yüan's three challenges illuminate the great gap we ordinarily experience between our so-called self and our bodies, words, and emotions.

The great Soto Zen master Dogen called the moment when that gap of separation disappears "body and mind dropping off." Who are you when your body and mind have dropped off? Wu-men's verse tells us that our body is not bounded by our skin but is one with the great body of the universe. We must function freely as part of this great body, unimpeded in any direction. If we treat this koan as nothing more than a riddle, we imagine we can easily solve it by "just lifting" a leg. Then, we will glibly bypass the real work we all need to do to truly unify our life in action, speech, and feeling. Sung-yüan never found a student who could answer his three questions to his satisfaction, and at his death he put his robe away without naming a Dharma successor. We should remember his high standards when we think we've "understood" his koan.

CHAPTER FIVE

SELF AND EMPTINESS

THE CONCEPT OF EMPTINESS has generated about as much confusion as oneness. In the psychoanalytic literature, *emptiness* commonly refers to a pathological feeling of inner hollowness or deadness that plagues many borderline and narcissistic patients. Kohut recognized that these patients' subjective feelings of emptiness correlated with a failure to develop or sustain a stable, cohesive self. But the emptiness to which a fragile, poorly structured self is prone bears little relation to the Buddhist use of the word. In particular, we must beware of equating the outbreak of such symptoms with the dissolving of the ego or self that is said to take place in meditation. More likely, they signal the traumatic disruption of an individual's selfobject world. Such disruption can occur, for example, when a hitherto idealized teacher suddenly does something—perhaps through an inadvertent failure of empathy—that shatters the student's view of her as a stabilizing, empowering figure. The student may then feel bereft and adrift in a hopeless empty depression, where practice no longer seems to make any sense. To continue to practice together effectively, the student and teacher must come to understand the nature of the disruption and somehow restore the selfobject bond. The temptation for the teacher is to avoid responsibility for the disruption and claim that the student is entering a valuable and necessary spiritual crisis.

This stance can lead to a dead end or worse. Breakdowns are not breakthroughs.

In the popular literature on spiritual practices, emptiness is sometimes used to describe a state of pure awareness, an alert mind that is momentarily empty of thoughts. In *Zen and the Brain,* James Austin, who is both a neurologist and a Zen student, has outlined in a formal and sophisticated way the phenomenology of the meditator's subjective experiences and correlated them with their various hypothesized neurological underpinnings. In his detailed account of the full range of levels of awareness and absorption, the mind is first quieted and then progressively emptied of any awareness of both external and internal sensory stimulation, including the usual awareness of time and space. These special states of "empty," concentrated attention are referred to as *samadhi* in the Buddhist literature. Such states of consciousness represent the greatest *discontinuity* between Zen and psychotherapy, and different teachers vary on the centrality they assign to them in producing lasting insight. In the Japanese Rinzai tradition they are seen as the necessary preludes to the sudden breakthroughs known as kensho.

But there is also another sense of "emptiness." Traditionally, emptiness is another way of speaking about impermanence. According to the Buddha, all *dharmas* (things or moments of experience) are empty of any fixed or essential nature. This lack of any individual essential nature can also been seen as another consequence of oneness—all dharmas are aspects of a constantly changing, co-determined, interdependent whole. To speak of the self as empty is to remark on the transience of all experience, without positing any permanent experiencer or observer set up in the background who watches it all go by.

When emptiness is used to convey impermanence, there is no one psychological state that corresponds to the "feeling" of emptiness, any more than there is a state of experiencing pure being. If I say an apple is round and red, how many attributes am I listing?

Does it possess *being* as an attribute in the same way it possesses redness and roundness? Could it have just the roundness and redness but not the being? To posit some intrinsic being or appleness alongside the apple's physical qualities of color, shape, and texture (and their constant, if ever so slight, physical changes) is to posit the sort of fixed, unchanging essence that the Buddha's teaching denies. Likewise, the *emptiness* of the self is not an additional attribute in any way on top of, behind, or between the gaps of moment-to-moment experience. It is not the silence between or behind our thoughts. It is just a way of saying that this moment-to-moment experience is all there is. Thus, in Buddhist terms, an awareness of emptiness is simply a nonresistance to the flow and transience of our lives. In practice, we watch where we resist letting things come and go. These nodes of resistance are what Buddhism refers to as attachment.

Nonattachment is an acceptance of impermanence. The tricky word here is *acceptance*. What does it mean to accept impermanence? Are we striving for a state of uncaring detachment? Surely not, for that would preclude compassion. Or do we imagine we can achieve a state of imperturbable equanimity? But that would put us back in the position of believing in some permanent, unchanging aspect of the self—the very thing that emptiness contradicts. Acceptance is nothing more than nonavoidance. Accepting the moment is simply a matter of experiencing the moment; as with emptiness itself, we're not adding any extra feeling of "acceptance" on top of the moment to make it feel different or better. I had a patient once who, whenever he had to go through some difficulty, even the unpleasant aftermath of prostate surgery, would try to "accept" what he was going through by adding "but that's OK!" to the end of his sentences. "I'm dribbling urine all the time. I have to wear a diaper to work—but that's OK, I can deal with it." Over and over, I'd interrupt him and get him to repeat the sentence back, leaving off the "that's OK." His attempt at acceptance was really a way to try to deny or hurry past his actual experience of difficulty. When he could stay with what was painful and humiliating to him about his problems, he came closer to genuine acceptance.

Robert Aitken Roshi, in an interview he gave at the age of eighty-three, talked about accepting change and dealing with loss: "If this house were to burn down and I were to lose my books and my archives, it would be a terrible blow for me. I would not easily be able to say, 'Well, everything is transient and I shouldn't be attached,' and all that kind of rubbish. I would really suffer."

The analysis of our resistance to change, of our unwillingness to face, accept, or mourn the impermanence or limitations of our bodies, relationships, or understanding, becomes part and parcel of what we literally sit with in the zendo. This way of understanding and practicing with emptiness and nonattachment—as opposed to a practice that focuses on states of samadhi—contributes to the *continuity* of Zen and psychotherapeutic practice. Here we might draw an analogy to the practice of free association. The traditional analysand was told to simply allow his or her thoughts to freely come and go, and to speak them aloud to the analyst without editing or censorship. Of course, resistance to this seemingly simple basic rule quickly sets in, and the nodes of resistance become the focus of further inquiry. In Zen practice, we might say, we allow not simply our thoughts but life itself to come and go.

The "Buddha nature" that Shakyamuni discovered that we all possess (whether we realize it or not) turns out to be not some innate, immutable spiritual essence—or even some innate potential for enlightenment—but impermanence itself. What would a life or a self that offers no resistance to its own impermanence be like? To fully accept the emptiness of experience, says Joko Beck, is to realize that "impermanence is, in fact, just another name for perfection."

What kind of perfection is this? Perfection is simply the full acceptance or nonseparation from life as it is.

HSI·CHUNG BUILDS CARTS

The Case

The priest Yüeh-an said to a monk, "Hsi-chung made a hundred carts. If you took off both wheels and removed the axle, what would be vividly apparent?"

Wu-men's Comment

If you realize this directly, your eye is like a shooting star and your act is like snatching a bolt of lightning.

> *Where the wheel revolves,*
> *even a master cannot follow it;*
> *the four cardinal half-points, above, below,*
> *north, south, east, west.*

In Chinese mythology, Hsi-chung was the man who first invented the cart. So this story starts off by asking us to look at what is true about carts from their very inception. Or, we might ask, what is the essence of a cart? With this metaphor, Yüeh-an is asking us to discover our own original nature or essence. If we take all the parts away, what is made clear about the essence of the cart? Is what is essential the wood from which its wheels and axles are made? But all the parts conceivably could be fashioned from some other material. Does a cart have to have four wheels, or could you design one with two or three? Is any particular configuration of the parts essential to its being a cart? A clever enough carpenter could probably improvise an alternative to any single part or arrangement you tried to single out as essential.

Or is it what the cart *does*? If so, if we say its essence is "carting," then we name an activity that constantly changes. What's put in the cart, how much of it there is, what it weighs, where it's taken and for whom may never be the same twice.

In Wu-men's verse, we read, "Where the wheel revolves / even a master cannot follow it." Its function, revolving, is continuous—*that* is inseparable into parts. Most of the time, we are all preoccupied with parts of ourselves or of our experience: parts of our personal history, parts of our self-image, parts of our body. And we are continually judging ourselves on how we think these various parts measure up to some ideal standard we carry around in our heads. We are proud of this part, ashamed of that part. We get so preoccupied with the parts that we lose sight of what our function in life is. Hsi-chung could have made his hundred carts in a hundred different shapes and sizes; what mattered was that in the end they could carry or haul what they had to. It's not easy to sum up in one word what our functioning is that is comparable to the hauling function of a cart, but *compassion* and *responsibility* are words Buddhists have traditionally used to express our most basic human functioning.

Aristotle described the soul using the metaphor of a candle. He said that our body was like a lump of wax and a piece of string; the soul was the arrangement of these into the shape of a candle with its wick. In this metaphor, the essence of the candle—its "soul"—isn't some additional thing added to wax and string, it is simply its functional organization: the assemblage of its parts in such a way that it can function in giving light. And what is particularly nice about Aristotle's candle, from a Buddhist perspective, is that once lit, a candle maintains its function even though its shape and size constantly change while it burns. In each moment the candle is slightly different from the way it was the moment before, yet the light remains steady.

Similarly, Hsi-chung's cart remains in constant use even while its various parts are continuously repaired, replaced, or transformed. That is how our lives go. Who we are, in terms of the *parts* of our lives, is in constant change; but all the while we function compassionately, responsibly using whatever is at hand. I first gave a talk on this koan a week after my mother died suddenly from a stroke. So part of who I was that day, part of my personal cart, was sadness. But I tried to integrate that event, and my response to it, into my overall functioning and use it as part of the ongoing exploration of life, which is my function as a teacher. Sadness gets woven into daily life the way my telling you about it is woven into the content of this chapter. None of this means we're supposed to keep functioning at any cost, ignoring our feelings. Ongoing maintenance, attention, and repair are all necessary to keep the cart functioning. The main thing is to stay willing, moment by moment, to incorporate everything that is at hand into the cart and then move with it in any direction—wherever our path takes us.

CHAPTER SIX

NO SELF

WHAT RELATION do individual moments of insight, those experiences of oneness or emptiness, have with the character structure of someone who is *enlightened,* when this word is meant to describe a completely selfless individual, someone we would call a buddha? Like the insights that occur in psychoanalysis or other disciplines, the insights of zazen offer us glimpses of a new way of being, a new experience of who we are. That way of being is one that makes none of our usual distinctions or separations. This transient moment, irrespective of its content, is perfect, just as it is. We might say that zazen gives us a momentary experience of *no-self* in place of the usual self-centered organization of experience. In the traditional koans, we sometimes hear a story that ends with the words "with this, the monk was enlightened." The temptation is to imagine those words are the Zen equivalent of "and he lived happily ever after." It's one thing to feel that a particular moment is perfect and quite another to imagine saying that about all possible moments. But that is precisely how Joko Beck describes enlightenment:

> If I am told, "Joko, you have one more day to live," is
> that OK with me?...

> If I am in a severe accident, and my legs and arms have to be amputated, is this OK with me?...
>
> If I were never again to receive a kind or friendly encouraging word from anyone, is this OK with me?
>
> If I make a complete fool of myself, in the worst possible circumstances, is this OK with me?

Her list goes on and on. But what does "OK" mean here? Not, she says, "that I don't scream or protest, or hate it or cry.... For these things to be OK doesn't mean I'm happy about them.... What *is* the enlightened state? When there is no longer any separation between myself and the circumstances of my life, whatever they may be, that is it."

Note that this absence of separation does not have any particular emotional state associated with it. OK-ness is not any feeling or affirmation added on top of the experience in question. She says she may hate it. This is what distinguishes Joko's "This is OK with me" from the OK-ing that my patient with the prostate problems was defensively trying to add on top of his painful experience.

There is no blissful glow of oneness here. An entire lifetime of engaged acceptance and functioning within the extremities of experience, such as the ones Joko lists, cannot be explained in terms of the afterglow of a single moment's realization. No single moment, no matter how profound, is going to bathe the rest of our life in sweetness and light, banishing any further discrimination or judgment. The oneness that is actualized in an enlightened life is not defined by a single moment of realization but rather by an engaged, wholehearted functioning. That functioning presupposes a cohesive structure of organizing principles through which to operate. In traditional Buddhist terms, we might see these organizing principles embodied in the Eightfold Path: the ongoing practice of Right

Views, Right Thought, Right Speech, Right Conduct, Right Liveli-
hood, Right Effort, Right Recollection, and Right Absorption. However we conceptualize them, such principles for moral action must
become thoroughly ingrained in our character; only then will kensho experience function in our action as wisdom and compassion.
The realization of nonseparation demands an *active* response to each
moment of life as it is—not a passive basking in the afterglow of a
moment of transcendental bliss.

Any insight, no matter how profound, requires a long period of
working through for there to be real character change. Otherwise,
we have simply had an intense experience, which quickly gets reified *as* an experience, and which we come to value precisely for its
specialness and the *discontinuity* between it and our ordinary life.

Part of the mythology of Zen, when I began my practice, was
that enlightenment experiences somehow would spontaneously dissolve all neurosis and that one would emerge from them cleansed
of all past conditioning. Nowadays, increasing attention is being
paid to what might be called "post-enlightenment practice." The
title of Jack Kornfield's book *After the Ecstasy, the Laundry* neatly
illustrates the dilemma of bringing grand spiritual insights down to
earth. Having interviewed nearly a hundred Buddhist teachers from
all traditions, Kornfield notes that a significant number have turned
to psychotherapy as a way of dealing with all those psychological
issues that enlightenment experience did not magically wash away.
Some teachers have been wise and humble about their need for help
with their all-too-human problems. Others, sadly infatuated with
their own attainments or narcissistically vulnerable to their students'
idealization and reverence, only acknowledged their limitations after
some personal crisis or misconduct forced them to confront the issue.

An infatuation with the intensity of kensho experience for its
own sake can be a particularly insidious form of Zen sickness.
Rather than using their insight as a light to illuminate the whole of

their lives, such individuals become Zen moths, uncontrollably and drunkenly drawn to their own light. Often students whose practice looks less spectacular but who continue on in a steady, seemingly uneventful way are more thoroughly and deeply transformed by their sitting. For them, practice is like going for a long walk on a foggy day. When we first set out, we may hardly notice the fine wet mist, but as we walk hour after hour, we finally arrive at our destination thoroughly soaked.

TRUE SELF OR NO SELF?

Whether we practice in the top-down style or the bottom-up, Zen offers us a perspective that is fundamentally nondualistic, anti-essentialist, and anti-transcendent. Furthermore, having achieved an experience of each of these states, Zen challenges us to demonstrate what it means to function from within them. We have seen non-dualism at work in Mu. The anti-essentialist perspective is further illuminated by a koan such as "This very moment, thinking neither good nor evil, show me your original face before the birth of your parents." The koan is posed in such a way as to engage our naïve assumption of an essential or true self, challenging students to work through all their preconceptions of who "deep down" they really are. Having gone beyond the dualism of father and mother, beyond "thinking good or evil," where do we find our essential true self? Hidden somewhere deep inside? Or right here, right now?

Buddha taught that the self is empty—that it has no fixed or essential nature. Rather than something hidden or esoteric, our true self is nothing more or less than what the opening words of the koan itself tell us: This very moment *is* our true self. Our original face can be none other than this moment's face. Finding out that you really are just *this*, nothing more than being *this moment*, may sound disappointingly ordinary or straightforward, and although the moment of realization may feel quite extraordinary, in the end, it truly is the most ordinary thing in the world.

Who we think we are "deep down," how we conceive of our essential nature, our "original face," is a problem with deep philosophical and psychological roots. Even when uprooted in a flash of insight, our self-centered view all too quickly reasserts its perspective. It is one thing to have a momentary realization of the emptiness of the self, and quite another to work through a lifetime of unconscious organizing principles and self-representations. Students commonly have momentary flashes of insight only to unreflectively return to their usual ways of being with all their ingrained sense of specialness, entitlement, or dependency intact. A psychoanalytically informed meditation practice will not allow a student to focus on the extraordinary moment of realization but will instead emphasize how such realizations go against the grain of the unconscious organization of day-to-day experience. Together the student and teacher need to watch out for all the ways in which the old patterns subtly seek to reestablish themselves while, at the same time, enjoying the new patterns as they take shape.

Eventually we come to realize that it is our very seeking for some imaginary pure or perfect inner essence that blinds us to the perfection of this moment. But the pull of "essence" is very powerful. Even Michael Eigen, a sophisticated psychoanalytic student of Buddhism, has mused that his British psychoanalytic mentors, Winnicott, Milner, and Bion, "would like the Zen koan, 'What was your original face before you were born?' because they all share a conviction that an original, naked self is the true subject of experience. Internalization processes are necessary for a fully developed, human self, but something originary [sic] shines through." Though Eigen normally is someone who celebrates a radical openness to the moment, here I'm afraid, he has fallen for the allure of an imaginary essence, searching for a chimerical true self that he assumes must be *behind* the moment and shine *through* it.

Toward the end of his life, the Trappist monk Thomas Merton came much closer to the mark when, looking back on his earlier writing about the "true self," he wrote in his journal,

> The time has probably come to go back on all that I have said about one's "true self," etc., etc. And show that there is after all no hidden mysterious "real self" *other than* or "hiding behind" the self that one is, but what all the thinking does is to observe what is there or objectify it and thus falsify it. The "real self" is not an object, but I have betrayed it by seeming to promise a possibility of knowing it somewhere, sometimes as a reward for astuteness, fidelity, and a quick-witted ability to stay one jump ahead of reality.

But one need not quote monks or mystics to illustrate the anti-essentialist perspective. In an article titled "A World without Substances or Essences," the American pragmatist philosopher Richard Rorty makes a very similar point. Pragmatism, he argues,

> break[s] down the distinction between intrinsic and extrinsic—between the inner core of X and a peripheral area of X which is constituted by the fact that X stands in certain relations to the other items that make up the universe. The attempt to break down this distinction is what I shall call anti-essentialism. For pragmatists, there is no such thing as a nonrelational feature of X, any more than there is such a thing as an intrinsic nature, the essence of X.

We suggest that you think of all objects in the following respect: there is nothing to be known about them
except an initially large, and forever expandable, web
of relations to other objects... There are, so to speak,
relations all the way down, all the way up, and all the
way out in every direction: you never reach anything
that is not just one more nexus of relations.

This sounds very much like a pragmatist version of the Buddhist
doctrine of *pratityasamutpada:* dependent co-origination or inter-
conditionality, which rejects the commonsense impression that
events possess a permanent, fixed being of an autonomous nature.

Lest we imagine this is a rather esoteric matter of only theoretical
interest, the Dogen scholar Francis Cook reminds us of some very
basic psychological implications of the anti-essentialist perspective:

Once we are able to perceive that there is change
only, and that we ourselves are part of the change,
there is no longer anything to possess, no me to
possess, no such thing as possession. Moreover, I
can understand that the impulses which torment
me and of which I am ashamed have no more solid-
ity and fixity than any other event. If anger, for
instance, were to possess any independent, real
existence, then I would be faced with a great problem, for it would exist in me apart from other internal or external causes, a constant personality defect
with which I would have to cope. However, since
anger is a momentary state arising from conditions
and then subsiding because of other conditions,
when it is gone, it is really gone, extinct. I am thus

not intrinsically an angry person, or a good person,
or any other kind of person.

Emotional essentialism is an often unnoticed component of many
psychotherapies and self-help programs. It commonly takes the
form of our being urged to "trust our feelings" or "listen to our gut
reactions." This way of thinking about emotion reduces it to a simple, unconditioned "inner voice" or a pure, intuitive responsiveness. But as I often tell students and patients alike, practice is a way
of learning to *distrust* our deepest feelings. (More crudely put, it is
a reminder that our guts are full of shit.) What we feel most deeply
or intensely may be our oldest, most thoroughly conditioned reactions. Sometimes, just because we feel our emotional reactions so
strongly, we are that much less inclined to recognize their idiosyncratic, conditioned, and subjective nature.

Who do you "instinctively" trust or distrust? What do you think
love is? When a patient tells me that she is in love, I never assume
I automatically know what she means. But if I ask too explicitly,
"What do you mean, 'in love'?" she may look at me as if I were crazy,
as if love were the most self-evident thing in the world. But does
love mean physical attraction? Feeling completely at ease with the
other person? Being able to trust that person completely? Feeling
perfectly understood? What if you feel intensely attracted to someone with whom you otherwise have nothing in common? Or trust
and feel completely at ease with someone you aren't attracted to? Is
it "really" love? We want to hold on to a picture of love as something
essentially simple and unambiguous, and we become confused
when its complexity and contradictions are revealed.

Sometimes we look to children to provide us with a model of
pure attention or complete absorption in the moment, and we fan-
tasize that practice will restore us to a state of lost simplicity or
immediacy. When I watch my son eat ice cream, it's easy to imagine

that his whole world is nothing but pure sensuous delight. But if I inadvertently put his ice cream in the wrong-colored dish or don't give him his favorite spoon or try to make him eat over a place mat, the picture changes. It turns out that his simple pleasure was not so simple after all. That "pure" childhood act is revealed to have many layers of opinion, likes, and dislikes already built into it (by age two!) that are required to make the experience just so.

The fact is, emotion is not simple. Emotional reactions are intimately tied up with our core beliefs and self-representations, a truth that was recognized not only by early Buddhist philosophers but by the Greek and Roman Stoics. Founded by Zeno of Citeum (335–263 B.C.E., not to be confused with Zeno of Elea, ca. 490 B.C.E., who is remembered for his paradoxes), Stoicism was an early and immensely influential attempt to untangle this relationship between reason and emotion. The philosopher Martha Nussbaum has noted that for the Stoics, "emotions are not simply blind surges of affect.... Unlike appetites such as thirst and hunger, they have an important cognitive element: they embody ways of interpreting the world." We should particularly note Nussbaum's use of the word *embody* here, and be sure to take it quite literally. One of the hallmarks of the Zen training I learned from Joko Beck is the emphasis placed on locating the bodily tensions that emerge during the course of our sitting as the physical correlates of our core hopes and dreads. Nussbaum continues,

> The feelings that go with the experience of emotion
> are hooked up with and rest upon beliefs or judg-
> ments that are their ground, in such a way that the
> emotion as a whole can appropriately be evaluated
> as true and false, and also rational or irrational,
> according to our evaluation of the grounding belief.
> Since the belief is the ground of feeling, the feeling

and therefore the emotion as a whole can be modi-
fied as a modification of belief.... [Specifically] the
beliefs on which our emotions are based promi-
nently include our evaluative beliefs, our beliefs
about what is good and bad, worthwhile and worth-
less, helpful and noxious.

In Buddhist terms, we might say that realization dissolves the
delusional, self-centered underpinnings of attachment.

In contrast with this nonessentialist approach to emotion common to both Buddhists and the classical Stoics, we should recall
that the hallmark of Freud's model of the mind was precisely his
postulating the existence of biologically predetermined motivational
impulses and fantasies that he called the *drives*. The Freudian id
was imagined precisely as a source of "blind surges of affect."

By formulating alternative, nonessentialist dynamic explanations
for subjective feelings of *drivenness*—accounts that do not rely on the
existence of underlying, universal, and permanent drives—self
psychology, intersubjectivity theory, and other relational models have
come around to a perspective far more compatible with Buddhist
models of the mind than was ever possible while the Freudian picture held sway. Rather than assuming the existence of, for example,
an immutable human tendency for aggression or destructiveness,
these new psychoanalytic models ask us to look into the specific contexts in which aggression arises. We then discover that narcissistic
injuries (i.e., traumatic blows to our self-esteem) often trigger aggressive responses. Different individuals will display varying degrees of
narcissistic vulnerability, and what counts as an injury may change
over time. With practice, the insult that once provoked rage can be
shrugged off. Our anger, rather than being a biologically predetermined part of our psyche, is a highly mutable, context-dependent
variable, one we can observe, understand, and ultimately transform.

DOGEN'S ENCOURAGING WORDS

In his brief *teisho* "Encouraging Words," Dogen quotes the maxim "Drop a coin in the river, and look for it in the river." What is the coin? What is it that you're looking for in this practice?

What is the river? The stream of consciousness, perhaps? Or the moment-to-moment experience of life as it is? What kind of coin can we pick out of that stream? Is the coin we find any different from life as it is, the stream itself?

What does it mean to drop the coin?

We've dropped the coin when we imagine our life is missing something essential, and we think we can find what we're looking for somewhere other than in our life right here as it is. This is how we all come to therapy, how we all come to practice: searching for something we think is missing from our lives.

If we look into the metaphor of the river a little further, and picture to ourselves a real river, we see that where we have to look may be quite intimidating. Not a quiet little pond, but a *river*—cold, swiftly flowing, deep, with a slippery, rocky shoreline. Looking in there may be cold and unpleasant at best, life-threatening at worst. Practice always means looking where we don't want to look, going where we don't want to go.

Remember the old joke about the drunk searching for his keys (or should we say his coins!) under a lamppost at night? Someone asks, "Is that where you dropped them?" And he answers, "No, but this is where the light is." Now, unfortunately, that's the way we often want to practice—where the light is. Not in the dark or down by the river. What is the light? It can be any state we're attached to—whatever we've privately decided a "good" sitting feels like. Calm, clear, quiet, joyful, whatever. And once we've practiced for a while, practice subtly becomes a project for getting into that special state and staying there as long as we can.

There's nothing wrong with such states, of course, but once you begin to practice this way, what I think of as real practice simply stops. When I ask students to describe their practice, they may say that they are "labeling thoughts" or "just sitting." On the surface, it sounds like everyone is practicing in the same, simple way. But once I get to know them individually, it usually turns out that they have a secret practice they don't want to talk about, a secret agenda for what they are trying to do or feel while sitting on the cushion. They don't want me to get wind of *that* practice, because they want to be left alone under their particular lamppost and not be pushed out into the dark.

Now there are a lot of meditation practices, particularly concentration practices, that are specifically designed to bring us some experience of that "light." And the danger is that we become Zen moths, endlessly circling the lamplight, fatally addicted to the brightness. Actually Zen students can be even worse than moths or drunks; they will sit around a lamp that once was lit months or even years ago, endlessly waiting for it to light up again. They sit waiting for a light they once saw in some sesshin or another, their whole practice devoted to trying to get that moment back, or even worse, remembering and savoring that moment over and over.

But real practice always takes place—out at the edge of the darkness. That's where we have to work. What is that edge? It's the boundary of where we feel comfortable, where the difficulties start. And that boundary is always clearly marked by anxiety or anger or fear: whatever we don't want to face. That's where we need to sit.

We all have to face the same basic difficulties. One person will come into *daisan* (an interview session) and say, "My knees hurt, my mind won't stop wandering, and deep down in my stomach there's a restlessness that just won't go away.... I'm having a terri-ble sesshin!" And then the next person comes in and says, "My knees hurt, my mind won't stop wandering, there's a terrible tight-ness in my guts—thank you for this chance to practice! I know that these are exactly the things I need to face!" That's the difference between looking for the light—trying to make all the difficulties go away—and knowing how to practice in the darkness, how to go down into the cold water groping for the coin. The coin is none other than our life as it is. We can find it anywhere—if we're will-ing to look for it everywhere.

CHAPTER SEVEN

THE MYTH OF
THE ISOLATED MIND

T HE REALIZATION of oneness (or nondualism) and emptiness (or nonessentialism) gives us a sense of our fundamental embeddedness in life, moment after moment. Dualism is
not just an abstract philosophical dilemma but a painful feeling of
alienation. Divided within themselves and never quite feeling at
home in the world, students and patients complain of feeling hol-
low, unreal, or as if they were "faking it." George Atwood and Robert
Stolorow, the founders of intersubjectivity theory, see this pervasive
alienation from lived experience as a consequence of "the myth of
the isolated mind." They identify three main areas of this alienation:

1. *alienation from nature,* including the illusion "that there is a
   sphere of inner freedom from the constraints of animal existence
   and mortality";

2. *alienation from social life,* including the illusion that each individual "knows only his own consciousness and thus is forever
   barred from direct access to experiences belonging to other people...which ignores the constitutive role of the relationship to
   the other in a person's having any experience at all";

3. *alienation from subjectivity,* including the "reification of various dimensions of subjectivity. These reifications confer upon experience one or another of the properties attributed to things on the plane of material reality, for example spatial localization, extension, enduring substantiality and the like.... Invariably associated with the image of the mind is that of an external reality or world upon which the mind entity is presumed to look out."

Dualistic pictures of self and other, self and world, body and mind, inner and outer have subtly permeated Western philosophy, including psychoanalytic therapy and theory. All of these dualities are directly challenged by Zen practice. Whether gradually, or in moments of sudden realization, Zen directly confronts and destabilizes our usual Cartesian presupposition of the essential interiority of the self—as well as any belief in a "true," "inner," or "essential" self or nature, all of which have been entangled with aspects of the myth of the isolated mind. The Zen alternative to a Winnicottian "false self" is not the discovery of an inner "true" self. But neither does it correspond to Kohut's own picture of a *nuclear* self, which one of his followers, Ernest Wolf, described in this way:

> At the time when an individual's self first comes into being as a singular and unique specific cohesive structure, the whole configuration of poles and tension arc being laid down is the core of this nuclear self. This unique core configuration gives the self an idiosyncratic and specific direction that in its lifelong unfolding can be called a life plan for the self.

According to this formulation, fulfillment comes from being in harmony with one's life plan, while failing to uncover or actualize this inner blueprint leaves one forever feeling unfulfilled.

Compare this to Joko Beck: "True self is nothing at all. It is the absence of something else." An absence of what? It is an absence, we might answer, not only of a "false self" but any notion at all of a "true self" or "life plan" that we seek to discover within our lives. The true self of Zen is *no self*: simply the immediate, non–self-centered response to life as it is.

How then should we understand the Buddhist concept of self-centeredness from a psychoanalytic perspective? I would offer this simple definition: *self-centeredness is the perspective of the isolated mind*. It is the perspective of someone who believes his or her self to be essentially private, interior, autonomous, and separate. In a half-joking imitation of Buddhist terminology, Stolorow has described the intersubjective alternative to the myth of the isolated mind as neither a one-person nor a two-person psychology, but a "no-person psychology."

When self-centeredness comes to an end, we discover not that our "self" has ceased to exist but that the self is not what we thought. The self is no longer an inner sanctum of private experience or a narrow set of personal needs or expectations. Our world is our self, rather than our self being our world. Rather than constantly trying to impose our self onto life, we realize that all of life is who and what we are. Or, as Dogen put it: "To carry the self forward and illuminate myriad things is delusion. That the myriad things come forth and illuminate the self is awakening."

What Buddhists have traditionally called compassion is simply whatever action or response flows from that awareness. A compassionate response will not necessarily look like kindness or niceness or anything else we may have in mind when we think of becoming "spiritual." (Think instead of all those old masters wielding a stick, spouting non sequiturs, or turning their backs on earnest students.) Indeed, compassion, like the self, is not any one thing at all.

WHAT NO-SELF IS NOT

Although we may have trouble saying just what a non–self-centered response to life looks like in any given situation, we can be clear what it is *not*. Non–self-centeredness is not what we ordinarily mean by self-effacement, and it certainly isn't masochistic self-sacrifice. I tell students that the Buddha's ideal of compassion does not mean dedicating one's life to saving all beings *minus one*. Alas, the language of no-self and selflessness is all too easily co-opted by our neurotic conflicts. Kohut taught us that when parents, out of their own emotional limitations, are unable to accept, and even joyfully respond to, the normal sexual and assertive feelings of their growing children, sexuality and anger become fraught with conflict. As children of such parents, we come to believe that such feelings are intrinsically bad or shameful and fear that their expression will lead to the disruption or withdrawal of parental love.

We may pursue spiritual disciplines as a way to expunge these frightening and dangerous aspects of ourselves. Sadly, we may turn to meditation as a form of psychological neutering. We may unconsciously strive to cut off our sexuality as a way to distance ourselves from early shame or abuse. We may try to purge self-assertiveness in order to negate the dangers posed by our own anger or the anger we were subjected to as children. All this may take place under the disguise of ever deepening calmness and a devotion to compassionate service. The blissful afterglow of samadhi is another favorite place to hide. I am always suspicious of students whose joyfulness or compassion looks too good to be true. A few rough edges are a sign of emotional honesty, while a totally calm and unruffled exterior often hides inner turmoil.

Fortunately, a growing number of therapists, themselves experienced meditators, are attuned to how patients may subtly distort Buddhist practice into a way of defensively denying pent-up anger or assertiveness. One such savvy therapist, Jeffrey Rubin, has written about his work with a patient he called Steven, a man in his mid-twenties who sought therapy as part of his "quest for self-development and perfection.... Although judged competent and successful by peers and students, he had anxiety about his capacities and often felt flawed and inadequate." With women, he often found himself in the "role of caretaker and...of healing wounded sparrows." From adolescence on, Steven had become "a kind of surrogate husband" to his anxious, conflict-avoidant mother, helping her cope with his troubled, drug-abusing younger sister. His hypercritical, perfectionistic father was subject to unpredictable, angry emotional outbursts. Steven strove to perfect himself through meditation practice in order to "compensate for his sister's difficulties and his parents sense of failure and to win his father's approval."

Rubin notes that for many years Steven's meditation practice was "focused on detaching from negative affects rather than experiencing them. This blocked the emergence of moral outrage against his parents for neglecting his needs and for allowing the disturbed sister to dominate family life. The possibility of Steven being appropriately assertive or angry was thus unfortunately stifled."

We see in this vignette how meditation was enlisted in the attempt to purge the self of the emotions that contaminated this patient's early family life: his sister's rebelliousness, his mother's neediness and anxiety, and his father's criticalness and anger. But by trying to use meditation as a practice of purification and purgation, these aspects of the self are simply repressed and never acknowledged and worked through. It is worth noting that what I would call Steven's misuse of meditation techniques in the service of his psychological defenses was never challenged by his meditation teacher, who evidently thought that Steven's progressive "detachment" from his negative emotions was a sign of progress. This is one case where it took psychotherapy to get meditation back on track.

No-self is the *whole* self functioning in a non–self-centered way. And we are able to function non–self-centeredly only when we are fully aware of the forces that pull us in the other direction.

NO TRANSCENDENCE

In the absence of a self-centered or isolated-mind perspective, our moment-to-moment functioning spontaneously manifests our natural embeddedness in life. This "true" self is neither inside nor outside; it is neither an inner life plan nor a union with a greater or transcendent Being. There is nothing "beyond" being just this moment. This realization illustrates the anti-transcendent aspect of Zen to which I alluded before. Putting an end to dualism and essentialism does not catapult us into a "higher" realm, though that may be the initial impression conveyed by a kensho experience. Ultimately, Zen puts an end to any conception of such a realm. *Enlightenment is precisely the thorough abandonment of any notion of enlightenment.*

To convey the radical force of this definition to American ears, I have sometimes said that the common goal of Zen and psychoanalytic practice is *putting an end to the pursuit of happiness.* Psychoanalysts recognize many variations on the fantasy of enlightenment —fantasies of immunity or detachment, immortality or uniqueness, perfect equanimity or freedom from emotionality. All represent ways the isolated mind imagines perfecting itself in its isolation. But as Stolorow and Atwood remind us, the isolated mind is a myth, and the mind's true nature, whether we are aware of it or not, is inter-subjective and interconnected. And what it is connected to and part of is a real and messy world. Awakening from a dream of isolation, we return in laughter and in tears to the one real world we have been part of all along. Happiness is no longer something to pursue, to be attained by acquiring something outside of ourselves, but is the natural by-product of *being ourselves*.

An old teacher once said, "Do not think you'll recognize your own enlightenment." He wanted us to understand that any experience we can recognize has already become reified; it has become something separate that we can define, possess, and even be proud of. Like silence, enlightenment can only be defined by what it is not. How do you tell someone what silence is? As soon as we speak, we have broken the silence. It can be shown, but how can we speak about silence, when our words destroy the very thing they seek to describe? In koan after koan, the master strikes the young monk almost as soon as he has opened his mouth to ask a question. The monk still thinks the truth he seeks can be summed up in the words of questions and answers; the master's blow is beyond all conceptualization. Any picture we have of the enlightened mind immediately violates its true nature. Just as the true self of Zen is the absence rather than the presence of something, enlightenment is not something we can be said to *gain* by practice. As Kodo Sawaki Roshi said, "gain is delusion; loss is enlightenment." What we lose are the boundaries between the self and the world. But those boundaries were never really there in the first place. What have we accomplished after all?

JUI-YEN CALLS "MASTER"

The Case

The priest Jui-yen called "Master!" to himself every day and answered himself "Yes!"

Then he would say "Be aware!" and reply "Yes!"

"Don't be deceived by others!"

"No, no!"

Wu-men's Comment

Old Jui-yen buys himself and sells himself. He brings forth lots of angel faces and demon masks and plays with them. Why? Look! One kind calls, one kind answers, one kind is aware, one kind will not be deceived by others. If you still cling to understanding, you're in trouble. If you try to imitate Jui-yen, your discernment is altogether that of a fox.

> *Students of the Way do not know truth;*
> *they only know their consciousness up to now;*
> *this is the source of endless birth and death;*
> *the fool calls it the original self.*

Do you think this old master is talking to himself? Or should we ask, who is it, really, that calls? And who is it that answers?

"Master!"

"Yes!"

"Be aware!"

"Yes!"

It sounds like a dialogue, but Jui-yen is speaking both parts. Is he just speaking his thoughts aloud? We are all used to the idea of an internal dialogue. So much of our time is wasted on the endless mental rehearsal of *I said*, *he said*, and *I should have said....* Voices from our past, of our parents perhaps, rise up to offer us praise or blame. We endlessly judge ourselves and give ourselves grades on how we're doing. But that's not what's going on here. Don't think Jui-yen is just spurring himself on to practice harder. This is not a dialogue between Jui-yen and his superego! But what happens when the internal dialogue comes to an end? Will you simply sit in silence? Jui-yen takes the stage to show us the next step.

One of the traps of practice is to think that it is something we do as individuals. We're good or bad at it; we do it conscientiously or lackadaisically. We treat it as our personal project or exercise. When we think of practice this way, we're inclined to view life as a series of oncoming events that practice teaches us to "cope with," "handle," or even "master." Then, when something difficult or traumatic happens, we wonder whether our practice is up to handling it. But practice is just being this moment. How could you be good or bad at it? How could you be anything else? But when we're lost in our self-centered dream we lose sight of this basic security.

Practice isn't a skill we cultivate "inside" us. In fact, as Jui-yen dramatically reminds us, the "self" isn't "inside" us at all! That's the mistake Wu-men's verse warns us against—confusing "the original self" with "consciousness up to now." What is the original self? Being just this moment—not *me* at this moment, but the whole of life manifesting right here, right now. Jui-yen's odd one-man show confounds our ordinary sense of inside and outside, of self and other. Playing both parts, or as Wu-men says, putting on angel faces and demon masks, Jui-yen makes a shambles of oneness and twoness. When the self is no longer confined to "me," it has a whole world of parts at its disposal.

At the end of every sitting, we chant: "Each moment, Life as it is—the only teacher." Life is the master to whom Jui-yen calls, and life is the teacher who answers. But there is no boundary between Jui-yen and life. Life calls; life answers life. Or, we might say, life takes the stage and plays at being Jui-yen. "Don't be deceived by others!" How can we be deceived by life? Only when we see ourselves separate from it, when we make a distinction between self and other. Don't be deceived. Don't think there is any place your true self does not reach.

Practice is nothing more than an ongoing awareness of this identity of ourselves and life. Life, if we can bear to listen, reminds us of this simple truth moment after moment. And it has an endless supply of voices at its disposal when it wishes to call out to us. Do you have an equal number with which to respond?

CHAPTER EIGHT

CONSTANCY

I'VE STRESSED the importance of functioning because it is central to another dilemma and misconception concerning the emptiness of self and the meaning of no-self. Buddhism teaches that the self, along with everything else, is empty, changing, and impermanent. How then do we account for constancy? These days I manage to visit my teacher Joko Beck in San Diego only once or twice a year, but when I visit, even though I know everything changes, there's something about her that I expect to be the same. For instance, I don't expect her to announce that she's given up Zen to devote all her energy to playing the stock market! If there's no permanent "self" that is Joko, what am I counting on? Perhaps some psychoanalytic perspectives on the self can contribute to the answer.

The relational analyst Stephen Mitchell noted that analytic theories tend to organize themselves around two fundamentally different perspectives on self-experience: the self is viewed either as relational, multiple, and discontinuous or as integral, separate, and continuous. Mitchell's own picture of the self as multiple and discontinuous, positing a succession of transient "selves" rather than a single unified self, does a good job of capturing the anti-essentialist, impermanent dimension of self-nature. But lacking any realization of intrinsic oneness or interconnectedness, Mitchell's version of multiple selves essentially constitutes a succession of isolated minds, each in a different "relational configuration." Each successive self, despite being "impermanent," remains self-centered in its perception, motivation, and functioning. Relational therapy is geared toward increasing the repertoire of available relational configurations or "selves" at one's disposal, and easing the grip of old, rigidified familial patterns of self-definition and relatedness. The capacity for multiplicity, to assume multiple roles or to assign multiple meanings to experience, becomes a value in its own right. However, it does not, in my reading, adequately address the potential for a radical reconfiguration of self-centered motivation in light of an awareness of interconnectedness and the realization of the essential emptiness of self-nature.

Self psychology's picture of the self as "integral and continuous" (in Mitchell's terminology) would seem better at accounting for the ongoing functioning of core values that persist even as self-centeredness drops away. But how does Zen reconcile the impermanence of the self with the experience of constancy? And given the recurrent scandals that have plagued American Zen centers in recent decades, can or should we expect any guarantee of a constant core of ethical values? If so, what is their relation to the impermanent self? Where else could they reside? Zen addresses this dilemma, I would suggest, in its own theory of unconscious process, a theory that both resembles and departs from the psychoanalytic picture of the unconscious in many significant ways.

Zen postulates a level of ongoing unconscious perception, understanding, and responsiveness that is separate from the self-centered concerns of the personal ego. This is part of what we are by virtue of being human, and is no more "personal" than the heartbeat or digestion. The Zen master Bankei (1622–93) referred to the *functioning* of this innate quality as the Unborn. I'm not equating the Unborn with the unconscious, you can be sure. The Unborn is not "inside" us; if anything, *we* could be said to be an aspect of *it*. The Unborn isn't something that has to be created or uncovered; it's what we (and everything else) spontaneously and naturally already are. Only our self-centeredness makes us unaware of its continuous natural unfolding and functioning. That functioning operates on what psychoanalysts are used to thinking of as a number of different levels, both perceptual and conceptual. Bankei's picture of the functioning of the Unborn challenges us to look at how we conceptualize what's *natural* for us as human beings. For instance, Bankei told his audience that the workings of the Unborn could be seen in the fact that:

> While all of you here are turned toward me, intent only on hearing my sermon and wondering, "What's Bankei going to say?" you aren't trying either to hear or not hear the cawing of the crows and the chirping of the sparrows out in back. But even so, once they start to chirp and caw, you recognize and distinguish the crow's *kaa-kaa* and the sparrow's *chuu-chuu*. And it's not only for crows and sparrows; everything here, when you perceive it with the Unborn, will be simultaneously distinguished and you won't overlook even one thing in one hundred or one thousand…. Your distinguishing everything you see and hear like this, without producing a single thought, is the marvelously illuminating dynamic function, the Buddha Mind that is unborn.

The Unborn doesn't operate just on the level of perception. Wisdom and compassion are innate human attributes that can function as spontaneously as sight and hearing, but these are especially liable to be interfered with or obscured by overlays of self-centered thought and delusion. Again, according to Bankei:

>All delusions, without exception, are created as a result of self-centeredness. When you are free of self-centeredness, delusions won't be produced. For example, suppose your neighbors are having a quarrel: if you're not personally involved, you just hear what's going on and don't get angry. Not only do you not get angry, but you can plainly tell the rights and wrongs of the case—it's clear to you as you listen who's right and who's wrong. But let it be something that concerns you personally, and you find yourself getting involved with what the other party says or does, attaching to it and obscuring the marvelously illuminating function of the Buddha Mind. Before, you could clearly tell wrong from right; but now led by self-centeredness, you insist your own idea of what's right is right, whether it is or not.

What would psychoanalysts make of Bankei's claim to be able to spontaneously tell right from wrong? Is that one of our "natural" human capacities? If so, in psychoanalytic terms, what kind of unconscious processes are involved in making such judgments?

Nowadays, few psychoanalysts think of the unconscious in purely Freudian terms as the repository of forbidden sexual and aggressive wishes. Instead, the unconscious is said to include a broad array of *organizing principles* that operate outside awareness to shape or structure our experience. We can use Bankei's sermon to illustrate aspects of what Stolorow and Atwood call the "pre-reflective unconscious" and the "dynamic unconscious." The latter, a repository of "expectations and fears," corresponds to intrusive self-centeredness in Bankei's example. It reflects our personal emotional experience—how we've learned to feel entitled, shameful, joyful, guilty, or frightened by our emotions in the course of grow-

ing up. The pre-reflective unconscious is a broader, more general-
ized, "spontaneous" organizer of experience. In addition to the
residue of our personal histories, it includes all those linguistic, cultural, and historical factors that also shape our perceptions. We can
spontaneously recognize the difference between a man and a
woman, but that distinction carries a whole array of connotations
and judgments that don't come into play when we differentiate
between a circle and a square.

No doubt, most modern-day analysts and philosophers would
say Bankei probably needed to be more cautious about what he took
to be "spontaneous" or "natural." As Gregory Bateson warned, the
surest way to be trapped by an epistemological system is to assume
that you don't have one and thus that you perceive reality "directly."
The theoretical and practical problem that faces us is whether we
can draw any clear boundary between those unconscious organizing principles that give rise to self-centeredness and those that "naturally" organize our experience. What we call our "gut reactions" are
all too often idiosyncratically colored by the dynamic unconscious,
as we saw in chapter 6.

Phillip Ringstrom, an intersubjective psychoanalyst, has suggested we make a further distinction between two types of organizing principles that make up the pre-reflective unconscious. The first,
invariant organizing principles, are "rigidified structures that impede
fluid engagement with one's surround." These are the habitual, dualistic notions we all carry around as personal and cultural baggage
and which are transformed to a greater or lesser extent in psychotherapy as well as Zen practice. (In Zen terms, these would constitute another unconscious level of self-centeredness.) By contrast,
variant, developmental, adaptive organizing principles remain open to
adaptation and change and spontaneous engagement with novel sit-
uations. Ringstrom especially prizes moments of intense spontaneous engagement "such as between lovers, an initial encounter

with a new infant, or in meeting a wild animal wherein the mutual curiosity of both human and animal overrides each one's fear." Chao-chou's placing his sandal on his head (see p. 96) is probably just the sort of improv Ringstrom would admire.

The psychoanalytic view of our subjective self-experience as inextricably intertwined with multiple layers of unconscious processes and organizing principles raises problems for Bankei's clear division between the self-centered "self" and a pristinely functioning "Unborn" that remains when self-centeredness gets out of the way. For Bankei, the unconscious organizing principles that form the basis of his spontaneous judgments of right and wrong aren't part of his notion of "self." And because they operate as spontaneously as seeing and hearing, there is no separation between their functioning and Bankei. In striking contrast to the emphasis that psychoanalysis places on the individual and subjective nature of our organizing principles, Bankei finds no permanent core of *personal* values or beliefs underlying our self-centered concerns; rather, we share a *universal capacity* for a natural, fluid, and compassionate responsiveness that is revealed when self-centeredness drops away. From an intersubjective, psychoanalytic perspective, no two people can ever hear the same birdsong. But in Zen terms, when we just listen, there is only the birdsong, no individual listener at all.

Bankei's Zen offers us a deep realization of our essential rightness and at-homeness in the world. Yet, a great danger awaits here, especially for teachers. Once one assumes that one is "enlightened"— that one's every response is a manifestation of unselfcentered "natural" functioning, then all further practice and inquiry into the unconscious roots of one's behavior comes to a halt. At its worst and most extreme, being "natural" makes a travesty of liberation and licenses outrageous behavior, including alcohol and drug abuse and the sexual exploitation of students. But even in the absence of such gross character pathology, history and experience show us that all of us, "enlightened" masters included, organize our experience through a multiplicity of culturally determined preconceptions about, among other things, race and gender, alongside our own personally conditioned core beliefs. None of these can be assumed to neatly and permanently drop off as part of a clearly demarcated layer of self-centeredness. The old Chinese masters famously freed themselves from traditional notions of social rank and decorum: Huang-po (known in Japanese as Obaku) is even said to have slapped the emperor. No doubt an enormous amount of cultural baggage drops away in the course of practice, but without an appreciation for the subtleties of the unconscious, we can fall into the trap of assuming that our newfound liberation is both total and final.

The temptation to believe that one is, at long last, just acting "naturally" can be particularly insidious. This is so because whatever is left over when a substantial chunk of our self-centeredness drops away has, if nothing else, the subjective *feel* of direct, unmediated experience—whatever a psychoanalytically or epistemologically sophisticated observer may say to the contrary. James Austin, who as a neurologist specializes in how the brain organizes and processes information, finds himself convinced that "the feeling that ultimate reality is being perceived constitutes *the raw data*" of kensho experience. Similarly to Bankei, Austin concludes that his experience "reveals innate neurophysiological capacities" and that he is touching the bedrock of perception and cognition. Perhaps it is only the isolated mind, preoccupied with its sense of separateness from the world, that worries about what epistemic filters it must be using in its struggles to reconnect with a split-off reality. If so, we may reap an unexpected benefit from that seemingly delusive perspective if it propels us to look beyond our subjective experience of immediacy and into our unconscious processes.

In the zendo, students are called to the morning's first sitting by the rhythmic sound of a wooden gong, the *han*, on which is inscribed a verse that exhorts them to be "like a fish, like a fool." Simply enter into the swim of things, never once thinking the word *water*. But as the old joke reminds us, whoever first discovered water, it certainly wasn't a fish, and being a fool about the milieu we live in may not be an unalloyed blessing. Bankei, like the fish, feels completely at home in his world. One might say there is a perfect fit between self and world in Bankei's Zen. This fit means we all have a natural embeddedness in life; there is no preexistent separation between self and world that needs to be overcome. The caveats about the dangers of presumed "naturalness" aside, there is something wonderfully simple, refreshing, and liberating in Bankei's Zen that is lost amid all the complexity and sophistication of the psychoanalytic model of the mind.

Compare Bankei's sense of at-homeness in the world with the world-view expressed in W.R. Bion's notion of intrinsic deficit, as described by his follower, Michael Eigen: "[Bion] calls on us to face the fact that our ability to process experience is not up to the experience we must process.... The deficiency in our equipment begins whenever processing of experiencing begins, a primary process deficiency. We can not keep up with experiential impacts.... Our equipment produces states it can not handle.... It is doubtful we can ever catch up with ourselves, or do ourselves justice, whatever level of processing we tap."

But as the contemporary poet and Zen teacher Philip Whalen has quipped, "Plenty of people will tell you that it is the Fate of Man to be eternally a day late and a dollar short. Don't you believe it!"

What changes in us and what remains constant in the course of practice is a vexing question, one we will return to in subsequent chapters. The simplicity of Bankei's answer has great appeal, but it may prove to be conceptually weak in light of our modern understanding of the complexities of the unconscious mind. For now, we can simply note that Bankei's answer to the riddle of my teacher's constancy—how come I'd be surprised if one day Joko quit Zen and took up day-trading?—would lie both in the consistent absence of something and in the consistent presence of something. What is consistently absent is intrusive self-centeredness. What is consistently present is a "spontaneous" responsiveness and functioning, so much a part of her "self" that she does not "possess" it or even experience it as part of herself. Bankei was right to point out how our capacities for responsiveness—starting at the level of simple sensory perception all the way up to complex moral and cognitive discriminations—can be experienced as part of a continuous, seamless spectrum of wholehearted functioning. And this functioning can proceed (by and large) quite independently from any self-centered or narcissistically invested sense of ourselves as the one doing it. Aitken Roshi sums it up for us in the simplest possible terms: "The self is still present—but it is not self-preoccupied. It washes the dishes and puts them away."

NAN-CH'ÜAN KILLS THE CAT

The Case

The priest Nan-ch'üan found monks of the eastern and western halls arguing about a cat. He held up the cat and said, "Everyone! If you can say something, I will spare this cat. If you can't say anything, I will cut off its head." No one could say a word, so Nan-ch'üan cut the cat in two.

That evening, Chao-chou returned from outside and Nan-ch'üan told him what happened. Chao-chou removed a sandal from his foot, put it on his head, and walked out.

Nan-ch'üan said, "If you had been there, the cat would have been spared."

Wu-men's Comment

Tell me, what is the meaning of Chao-chou putting his straw sandal on his head? If you can give a turning word here, you will see that Nan-ch'üan's challenge was not irresponsible. But if you cannot yet do this—danger!

> If Chao-chou had been there
> He would have taken charge;
> He would have snatched away the sword
> And Nan-ch'üan would have begged for
> his life.

Let's begin with the arguing monks. If we're going to make this old story relevant to our practice, we have to begin by acknowledging that we act more like them—bickering much of the time—than like either Nan-ch'üan or Chao-chou! Even when we're not arguing with one another, our heads are filled with arguments: about what's right or wrong, true or false, fair or unfair. Back and forth, to and fro, we fill our heads with that endless internal dialogue.

So let's not dismiss the arguing monks too quickly, but instead try to imagine what they're arguing about. Sometimes it's said they're arguing about whether the cat has the Buddha nature or not, but that's not something most of us can imagine getting too worked up about. I like to imagine they are arguing over the ethics of keeping a cat in a monastery. As good vegetarian Buddhists they don't want to voluntarily kill any sentient beings, but mice are eating up their rice supply! Is it ethical for monks to keep a cat to do their killing for them? That might provoke a heated argument in some places even today. Now maybe we can empathize with them a little and not just see them as foils for Nan-ch'üan and Chao-chou.

So Nan-ch'üan comes upon the argument, and what he sees is the endless to-and-fro; all the monks caught up in the dualism of right and wrong. Can he get them to see from another perspective? He demands they "say a word" or he'll kill the cat. What does "say a word" mean?

I'm reminded of a scene in one of J.R.R. Tolkien's books where Gandalf and company have come upon an enormous stone gate blocking their way through the mountains. On top of the gate is an inscription carved in some old half-forgotten language that Gandalf thinks can be translated, "Say the word, friend, and enter." So Gandalf tries every secret password and magical spell he can think of, trying to say the word that will open the giant gates. All to no avail. Then, finally, he realizes the inscription says, "Say the word *friend* and enter." The "secret" word was written right there in front of him all along.

But none of Nan-ch'üan's monks can say a word and he kills the cat. Is it fair to kill a living creature just to make a dramatic point? A fair question, but one that will toss you right back into the midst of the monks' original argument.

That night when Nan-ch'üan tells Chao-chou what happened, Chao-chou immediately puts his sandal on his head and walks out. What do you make of that? How is putting your sandal on your head "saying a word" of Zen? The danger here, of course, is thinking that Chao-chou's gesture has some deep, esoteric "Zen" meaning. People have interpreted that gesture in all sorts of ways. Some say it's a way of illustrating how topsy-turvy the arguing monks' thinking was. In his commentary on the case, Aitken Roshi says that in old China putting your sandals on your head could be a show of mourning. Maybe a Catholic would automatically make the sign of the cross when hearing about the poor cat. Whatever it "means," it was simply Chao-chou's spontaneous response to the story, and the immediacy of that response stands in stark contrast to the garrulous monks who stand speechless when asked to "say a word."

Traditionally, Nan-ch'üan and Chao-chou are said to each wield a sword: Nan-ch'üan the sword that kills, Chao-chou the sword that gives life. Nan-ch'üan's sword cuts through all thought, all dualism. Nothing is left. What then? Chao-chou shows how we must respond from that place of no thought. It's not enough to empty our heads of dualistic thinking; we must act.

One of the things I like about beginning a sesshin by chanting the Heart Sutra and the *Sandokai* in their Sino-Japanese versions, as well as in English, is the way that makes us concentrate on them as pure sound. You must concentrate fully on just making a sound, with no room for any thought about what it means. If you think about it, you're lost. With all our attention on those "nonsense" syllables, there's no room for a thought in our heads. And yet our attention is sharp and we chant vigorously and in unison. Our whole day needs to be like that. We label our thoughts as "thought" and see them as the background noise of old monks arguing, arguing. We come back, without thought, to awareness of breath and body and all the sounds that penetrate the zendo. But we can't disappear into that "thoughtless" place—at any moment we have to be prepared to act, to pay attention to how we bow, how we walk, how we do *oryoki,* how we work. We must continually be ready to "say a word."

CHAPTER NINE

CHANGE

ZEN'S ATTACK on self-centeredness demands a radical transformation of our isolated minds both at the level of conscious, subjective experience and at the level of the pre-reflective and dynamic unconscious. In Kohut's self psychology, structural deficits in the self are healed when *compensatory structure* is established based on new non–self-centered values and ideals, which then form the basis for "spontaneous" compassionate responsiveness. Working from within a neo-Freudian ego psychology, W. W. Meissner has referred to the process of fundamentally restructuring the ego ideal as "transvaluation." However we conceptualize it, a radical transformation of self-organization occurs. Meissner was, I believe, correct to emphasize the "constructive and synthetic" aspect of this process, rather than to focus solely on the collapse or dissolving of old structures.

Psychoanalysis tends to view old patterns of organization as something to be gradually outgrown or moved beyond developmentally. Zen, on the other hand, is more likely to directly confront and challenge the old patterns or organizing principles that constitute our self-centeredness. The difficulties inherent in Zen practice (the emotional and physical stress of long hours of sitting) and the conceptual quandaries that arise by having our usual frame of reference radically challenged by the seeming incomprehensibility of a nondualist, nonessentialist perspective as encapsulated in koans—all combine to undermine preexisting modes of organizing and mastering experience. In this sense, the experience of *not* being able to answer a koan may be as important as finally answering it. One's self-image and self-importance, along with all one's usual modes of knowing, may be threatened or undermined in the face of a seemingly unsolvable koan. A story (perhaps apocryphal) that made the rounds in one Zen center told of a student so enraged by the roshi's repeated refusal to accept his answer to his koan that he threw himself on the teacher and tried to strangle him! Who was the student? A famous psychoanalyst!

Deliberately placing difficulty in the path of the student has always been a central part of Zen training. Meanwhile psychoanalysis seems to be moving in the opposite direction. Self psychologists have gradually backed away from Kohut's own notion of "optimal frustration" and toward a more nurturing stance of "optimal responsiveness." Perhaps the example of Zen can remind analysts that the optimal response may sometimes take the form of a difficulty that challenges or disrupts old patterns of organization.

A BIGGER CONTAINER

For the dismantling of old structures of subjectivity to result in a breakthrough rather than a breakdown, the student must have basic skills of *affect regulation* at his or her disposal. This simply means the capacity to tolerate, endure, and meaningfully organize one's emotional experience, so that one isn't overwhelmed by the anxiety, pain, uncertainty, or other reactions stirred up by sitting. In the absence of this capacity, a student may panic, feel pointlessly or sadistically tortured by painful sitting, or evolve quasi-delusional grandiose fantasies of enlightenment as a way of making sense of what's happening.

Zen has traditionally tended to take these affect-regulating capacities for granted as the by-product of individual discipline and effort, part of the basic level of maturity expected of a monk. Looked at from a psychoanalytic perspective, we can begin to say more about the intersubjective context in which affect regulation develops through meditation.

Most of the changes that result from meditation practice derive not from dramatic so-called enlightenment experiences but from the slow, structure-building aspects of sitting itself. There are many parallels between psychoanalysis and meditation in the way these capacities are developed. Like analysis, meditation practice creates a long-term relationship with a figure who serves a positive self-object function, as well as becoming the object of transference longings and expectations. Like analysis, meditation practice creates a setting for the eliciting and working through of intense fantasies and affects. Like analysis, meditation trains us to stay with, tolerate, and explore thoughts and feelings normally felt to be too painful or frightening to endure. I call this the *structure-building* aspect of practice. By "structure," I simply mean the capacity to tolerate and meaningfully organize our emotional experience. The absence of this capacity is reflected in the subjective sense of being overwhelmed by experience or of intolerable anxiety in the face of certain feelings, all of which may lead either to the unconscious repression of the dreaded thought or feeling or to conscious avoidant behaviors. Another manifestation of this insufficiency is the subjective experience of inner emotional emptiness or deadness, which can lead either to an immobilizing depression or to compulsive, addictive attempts at self-stimulation.

Meditation teaches us to literally sit with and through all of these states in a way that progressively builds our capacity to tolerate, regulate, and organize our affective experiences. There is nothing mystical about this aspect of practice. The first rule of a sitting practice is *to sit still*. That means sitting still through restlessness, not scratching itches, not wiping a dripping nose, not moving a foot that has fallen asleep or is in pain. Beginners will often feel close to panic at the thought of following this simple rule. They may have a frightening feeling of being trapped or of going stir crazy when they think of being unable to respond to such basic aversive cues.

Meditation offers many such challenges. Long periods of it can be physically painful. It can be boring. During long hours of sitting our mind wanders repeatedly, drifting in characteristic patterns. Whatever happens, whatever we feel, we learn to stay with it, observe it, feel it. Joko Beck has called this structure-building aspect of practice "building a bigger container." As my teacher, Joko demanded nothing more or less than emotional honesty from me. Over and over she emphasized that practice is not about becoming somebody else, or attaining any particular state, but rather settling deeply into the physical and emotional reality of this moment. She asked her students to be attentive to the emotional or affective coloration of each moment: Where, she might ask, is that feeling in your body? Is there a tension or tightness in your throat, your neck, your belly, as you allow yourself to fully feel this moment? Can you feel the resistance to fully being present that is manifesting as that bodily tension? Practice for Joko meant learning to sit with resistance, to identify resistance in the form of bodily tensions, to plumb the emotional history of those tensions, moment after moment.

When we sit, we do not try to become calm or peaceful or to quiet the mind, but rather, we practice staying with and amid whatever feelings arise. Simply sitting still for regular periods of time every day does, however, have a steadying and centering effect. Following the breath and labeling thoughts builds a stable internal "observer" who is not buffeted by conflicting emotions or swept away by the flow of association or rumination. A meditator becomes increasingly able to interrupt repetitive or obsessive trains of thought and sit with the anxiety or bodily tension that ordinarily accompanies such thinking in an inner, wordless silence. At this point, the "observer" dissolves into the experience of just sitting. It is this increasing capacity to tolerate previously intolerable, warded-off affect states that provides the core structure-building dimension of Zen practice. Like psychoanalysis, Zen practice is a *structured, relational context for eliciting, tolerating, and working through one's patterns of affective experience,* including affects that have been previously repressed or dissociated. The long hours of physically difficult sitting, the relationship to an idealized teacher, and the student's own expectation of transformation are powerful elicitors, both of selfobject transferences that gradually strengthen and stabilize the self and of old, repetitive patterns of thinking and acting that need to be challenged. Furthermore, the group context of practice can elicit strong twinship transference experiences that help the individual to feel that what he is going through is a shared, understood, and bearable form of difficulty, even when at its most extreme. All this contributes to an increased capacity to contain and stay with hitherto states of physical and emotional pain, uncertainty, and disorientation as old dualistic patterns of organizing one's sense of self and the world arise during sitting practice.

THE INTERSUBJECTIVE CONTAINER

In Zen, unlike psychoanalysis, it is not primarily the sense of feeling understood by another person that provides the container for affect. Rather, an individual's capacity for affect tolerance and regulation is strengthened by sitting within the enabling selfobject context of the group as well as by the student-teacher relationship. This Zen container provides what psychoanalysts would call the "affect-integrating, containing, and modulating intersubjective context" that allows previously dissociated traumatic affects to be safely re-experienced and worked through. Dualism manifests in our emotional life as dissociation from our own experience. No spiritual practice can truly undo a dualistic perspective without engaging and working through previously dissociated emotions. Otherwise, momentary experiences of "oneness" will only serve to further split off and sequester dissociated traumatic affects with a false promise of attaining a transcendent state beyond the reach of the old trauma.

From the perspectives of self psychology and intersubjectivity, psychoanalysis cures by "providing missing developmental experiences"—what Kohut originally meant by selfobject transferences—and by providing "responses from the analyst that counteract invariant organizing principles that are manifestations of...the repetitive dimension of the transference." As I have tried to indicate, Zen training tacitly provides powerful selfobject experiences without ever, or only rarely ever, explicitly acknowledging their role. In the past, such provisions would simply be part of the expectable background of monastic life. In a modern, psychoanalytically informed Zen practice, the selfobject dimension of the student-teacher relationship can be more directly addressed.

The invariant organizing principles that are manifestations of repetitive transference correspond largely to what Buddhism refers to as "self" or "ego," terms that have been used interchangeably over the years in translations of Buddhist texts. That the Buddhist and Freudian concepts of the ego are not congruent should by now be evident. The Buddhist goal of dissolving the ego doesn't imply aspiring to a loss of toilet training. The Buddhist version of self contains elements that pertain to our subjective sense of personal mastery and to our sense of ourselves as knowers, as well as to patterns organized around our sense of defectiveness or deficiency. Even though self-centeredness in the long run is the root of our suffering, nonetheless it retains a powerful short-term appeal! To challenge the hold of our self-centeredness, we must face the anxiety and doubt it keeps in check. How can we recognize these patterns in ourselves and what does it take to change them?

Our unconscious organizing principles most clearly reveal themselves when we find ourselves stuck imagining that our happiness is conditional on having a certain kind of experience, on being or becoming a certain kind of person, or on being treated in some special manner. Zen teaches us that, paradoxically, it is just when we become most hopeless about having those unconscious conditions ever being met, whether by attaining kensho or becoming someone other than who we already are, that we can find ourselves overtaken by a simple, joyful exhilaration at just being fully alive in the moment. Consider old Hsiang-yen who, unable to answer his teacher's question about his original face, resigned himself to leaving the monastery and becoming the caretaker of a nearby tomb. Lost in raking the leaves, his broom swept up a pebble that struck a nearby stalk of bamboo with a little sound—*tock!* Just then his original face was apparent to him.

Practice allows us to discover that our happiness is not dependent on any of the things we once thought so crucial. The old organizing principles that forever were warning us, "Do it this way or else!" are suddenly found irrelevant. Life offers us the unexpected pleasure in our own aliveness, vitality, and responsiveness. Being just this moment, we learn that we don't have to become anything new or somehow jettison all those shameful parts of ourselves in order to partake of this newfound bounty.

In psychoanalytic treatment, the grim, unconscious expectations of our core beliefs are counteracted by the *novelty* of empathic responsiveness. Our initial expectations of misunderstanding and mistreatment or a covert demand for compliance as the price of relationship are gradually dissolved by being related to with unexpected empathy and understanding. For a long time, though, we may remain hypervigilently attuned to any sign that the analyst has intentionally or unintentionally done something to confirm our old fears and expectations. In a successful analysis, however, we slowly allow ourselves to be pleasantly surprised by the possibility of a genuinely new kind of relationship. In psychoanalysis, the repetitive therefore tends to be viewed as synonymous with old patterns of organizing experience, schemas that the analyst hopes will gradually give way to more flexibility as the patient abandons old conceptual boxes. In the psychoanalytic view, existing organizing principles undergo alteration when new experiences disconfirm old unconscious negative expectations.

Zen and psychoanalysis both acknowledge the repetitive nature of a self-centered mode of organizing experience. But whereas both Zen and analytic approaches employ novel experience to disrupt old patterns, traditionally Zen has more affinity for the stick than the carrot. Consider the seemingly outrageous behavior of Zen masters in the classic koan collections. Receiving a sudden whack with a stick may be incomprehensible to a young student. (Some students, no doubt, found such arbitrary mistreatment all too familiar.) But in a moment of complete incomprehension, where everything we know or expect suddenly no longer makes sense, we may be able to experience everything afresh. Not understanding a single thing, we are nakedly present in the moment. Three times Linji asked his teacher to tell him the great essential truth of Buddhism, and three times his teacher hit him. Only later did he realize that those blows weren't punishment—they were the answer!

IN PRAISE OF REPETITION

Zen views repetition in a different light from psychoanalysis. Psychoanalysis has traditionally thought about repetition in terms of *internal* schemas we repetitively impose on the *outer* world, thus making the potentially new yet another replay of the past. For Freud, the compulsion to repeat negative past experiences operated at the deepest, most biologically determined levels of the psyche, levels that were unreachable by the classical psychoanalytic investigation of erotic conflict. More relationally minded analysts think of repetition as recreating the safe haven of those early nurturing relationships that we long to reinstate in the present, even at the price of infantalizing ourselves in the process. The repetitive and the therapeutic seem to be diametrically opposed.

But Zen fights fire with fire. Repetition itself is used to wear down old repetitive patterns of thought. This is possible because the old patterns are by their nature essentially self-centered. They inevitably contain expectations of what the self-centered mind wants, namely, experiences that reconfirm its own existence or importance, or that provide ongoing stimulation or a sense of specialness.

Like zazen itself, repetitive, ritualized practice or work continually goes against the grain of our self-centered expectations. Rather than being able to make our own distinctive mark or personalized statement in the way we do things, ritualized repetition erases any trace of our separate, particular contribution. When we get up from our cushions at the end of a day's sitting, we smooth them out so no trace of our having been there remains. The day-in, day-out routines of practice, whether sitting long sesshins or simply riding the subway, allow us to use repetition to wear down our craving for novelty and excitement. A psychologically minded practice keeps us attuned, not only to our usual reactions to routinized work but to our deeper underlying expectations of how we feel or think about ourselves, all of which provoke resistance to staying with the moment's activity.

Awareness of our expectations and resistances turns work into *work practice*. Our self-centeredness gradually withers in the midst of routines that offer no reinforcement to our ego's most basic demands for attention and specialness. When we find our chores boring, we can watch and label our resistances and finally surrender to the physicality of simple action—washing the dishes, riding the subway. At some point, we stop trying to make it interesting, and settle into body, breath, and motion. When our self-centered expectations of being entertained finally get out of the way, we may find ourselves surprised by joy in the midst of the ordinary and the routine. Then all those activities that our self-centered minds once labeled drudgery become part of the samadhi of everyday life. Indeed, as Dogen promised, "all the myriad things come forth" to awaken us to life.

I admit that I am painting a rather idealized portrait of the role of repetition in practice, largely to counterbalance the purely pejorative connotation it has acquired in psychoanalytic thinking, where repetition remains associated with stereotyped behavior or thinking. But Zen teachers must also be willing to acknowledge the danger of work practice degenerating into forced labor. Mere drudgery is no path to enlightenment. We practice using simple, repetitive work to free us from a restless craving for novelty and excitement, not to stifle our intellect or creativity. Especially in monastic communities, there has been the risk that everyone, regardless of their aptitudes or interests, is enlisted in the often exhausting physical labor of running some community business that supports the monastery but runs roughshod over the needs and limitations of individual practitioners. Such cases of work practice gone awry are particularly pernicious when objections to mind-numbing labor are dismissed as just so much egotistic attachment.

These caveats aside, work practice remains an integral part of every form of Zen practice, regardless of denomination, whether lay or monastic. It is the most basic expression of how our practice comes off the cushion and enters our lives. Years ago at the San

Diego Zen Center, I recall, everyone was invited to say a few words about the difference practice had made in their lives. The first few speakers spoke earnestly of the psychological changes they had experienced over the years, their increased patience, compassion, self-awareness, and so on, but then one woman brought the house down by saying simply, "My apartment is much cleaner!"

SITTING WITH SAM

After I had been a parent for all of three months, I felt I was enough of an expert to give a talk on the subject. Not that I'm an expert on *babies*—those few months taught me one lesson after another about how little I knew. In fact, one of the reasons my wife and I felt comfortable leaving Sam in the care of various baby-sitters a couple of nights a week was that it immediately became obvious how much more experience they all had with babies than either of us. No, what I've become an expert in is the many ways a little baby can make a parent feel—proud, frustrated, loving, exasperated, and so forth. And it's all these feelings that one time or another I've had to sit with when sitting with my son.

I say "sit with him" because of the particular role within the family I was assigned in those early days. My wife, who was staying home and breast-feeding, naturally bore the brunt of the work. I changed my share of diapers, of course, but there's no denying she was the one who had to deal with him alone most of the time. My special role came in the evenings or late at night, particularly when Sam had been having a rough day, maybe because of gas or overstimulation or whatever, and was crying inconsolably. When nothing seemed to quiet him down, I took over and held him in my arms and just sat with him while he cried. What I learned was that at some point I had to stop trying to calm him down or make him stop crying and be willing just to hold him while he went through whatever it was he was going through. Sometimes I'd gently chant *Mu-u-u*. I'm told low droning sounds, like a vacuum cleaner or running a tap, can quiet a baby, so maybe Sam found *Mu-u-u* soothing. Anyway, it certainly calmed *me* down and helped me sit with him.

You might say that I could just as well have put Sam in his crib and let him cry. But somehow, I think it made a difference that I was holding him, even when it didn't seem to do much immediate good.

I think what we're practicing in the zendo is something very similar. We all come in with one kind of distress or another: pain, confusion, buzzing thoughts. And what we do is sit with it. The structure of formal sitting, the posture of our bodies, our motionless silence, the quiet presence of those around us, all hold us while we sit with our distress. And just as there is a difference between letting a baby cry all alone and holding him, so it makes a big difference in our lives whether we thrash around alone with our pain or develop a formal discipline, either zazen or psychoanalysis, that allows us to contain it, observe it, and sit still in the midst of it. We learn to stop our frantic efforts to escape or fix our distress; we watch the thoughts of blame or explanation that arise around it, and we simply try to feel it and be with it. Practice becomes a container for our pain. And gradually, who we are becomes as much about being that container as it is about being preoccupied or identified with the pain.

Eventually, Sam would quiet down and fall asleep, sometimes within a few short minutes, sometimes only after being up most of the night. Whatever the night brought, we went through it together.

CHAPTER TEN

ZEN IS USELESS

IN THE PREVIOUS CHAPTER we discussed ways of thinking psychoanalytically about how character is transformed through Zen practice. We also have looked at how Bankei explained the continuity of core values and other natural capacities in the midst of an impermanent self, and how psychoanalysis would conceptualize the unconscious processes involved in the functioning of those capacities. But it isn't only ethical values and compassion that endure; problems of all kinds persist as well, and the disappearance of self-centeredness in our lives is never total or once and for all. Practice may utterly transform our lives in one dimension, while much about who we are in other ways may not change at all. In this chapter, we will inquire further into what changes and what doesn't, and the dialectic between acceptance and effort in our lives and in our practice.

Zen practice involves uncovering our core beliefs—especially our core beliefs about the nature of practice and what we expect to gain from it. Even though we may recite countless times the line in the Heart Sutra that tells us there is "no path, no wisdom, and no gain," each of us, in our own self-centered fashion, holds on to some hope, some picture of what we expect to gain from all this practice that we're putting so much time and effort into.

Now certainly we might argue that there are some seemingly straightforward rewards of practice. Generally speaking, we may become somewhat calmer; we may build up our capacities for concentration or endurance; we may become steadier and more reliable as a result of the rigors and discipline of the zendo. But if practice isn't about attaining any of these modest rewards, let alone the ultimate reward of kensho, why do we continue?

Uchiyama Roshi recalls, as a young monk, asking his teacher, the powerful and charismatic Kodo Sawaki Roshi, whether practice would eventually make him a little stronger. But Sawaki Roshi shouted, "No! Zazen is useless. I am not like this because of my practice of zazen. I was like this before I began to practice. Zazen doesn't change a person. Zazen is useless."

One couldn't ask for a more forceful presentation of "no gain." But if zazen is truly useless—if it has no goal outside of itself—what function is it serving? Why should we make the effort?

Dogen's great realization was that zazen is not a means to an end. Rather, practice is the endless expression of who we are. This is a subtle point, one that is easily misconstrued. But it goes to the heart of the problem of the motivation to practice. A few analogies may help clarify the issue. Imagine a person who is constantly dieting and exercising because he thinks he is fat. For him, constant effort is required to hold a dreaded aspect of himself at bay or to actualize a self-image of fitness or attractiveness. Compare the way he exercises with another person who also exercises every day, but who doesn't even own a scale. Even though this second person doesn't think working out will ever give her a perfect body, exercise simply feels like a natural part of her day. Somehow, her daily practice makes her feel "more like herself." Or consider a scholar who continues to study the latest research in her field—not "to keep up" or out of fear of missing some new development, but simply because study is an ongoing exercise of her talents and interests. We might say that studying is inseparable from who she is. No idea of gaining anything is necessary to provide the motivation to continue. This is Dogen's fundamental approach to zazen. To sit is to be who we are. We don't sit in order to become Buddhas or even to become more fully ourselves. Dogen invites us to extend this perspective beyond the functioning of any single activity—even sitting—to the whole of life itself. There is no "becoming someone" at all. We are our own endless and perfect expression of ourselves, of this moment, of life.

Being who and what we are, we find putting out effort comes as naturally as breathing. Self-centered ideas of gain actually intrude on our natural functioning and frustrate our experience of its spontaneous unfolding. At the same time, who we are is not static and unchanging. Exercise, study, and sitting will all have effects on our lives. We are the ongoing sum of our actions. To see ourselves and our practice this way dissolves the distinction between acceptance and effort. Effort *is* the acceptance and exercise of our true nature. Only when our understanding of this essential unity breaks down do effort and acceptance feel opposed to each other, and our practice becomes unbalanced. Effort without acceptance leads to becoming mired in loss and gain. Acceptance without effort ends in complacency.

The assertion that "zazen is useless" undermines any hope of gain and demands that we fully accept who we are at this very moment. Yet might not ingrained character flaws and unconscious patterns of thinking also hide behind such a stance? Like Bankei's sense that the Unborn spontaneously recognizes right and wrong, the idea that Zen leaves us with our own "natural" character will rightly sound suspicious to psychoanalysts. One way psychoanalysis traditionally classified patients' symptoms was on the basis of whether they were *ego dystonic* or *ego syntonic*—that is, whether a symptom caused the person distress or whether it was so integrated into the personality as to be noticeable to an observer but not to the patient himself. Phobias exemplify ego dystonic symptoms in that they are the source of the acute anxiety that drives a person into treatment. At the other extreme are psychopaths who have no subjective experience of distress and whose psychopathology is defined by its effects on others. Addictions like alcoholism may, for a long time, occupy a middle ground: the consequences for both the individual and others may be denied for extended periods of time and only gradually or after "hitting bottom" will the individual come to acknowledge there is a problem at all. True practice promises no gain, but how can we ensure that "no gain" doesn't become a rationale for denial?

We must be wary of too readily drawing any sharp line between where self-centeredness stops and who we "naturally" are begins. It is sobering to learn that Sawaki Roshi was one of several Japanese masters who vigorously supported his country's military efforts in World War II and who argued that the precept of not killing was not violated by those who threw themselves wholeheartedly into battle. The world will not conveniently divide itself into scoundrels and saints, and even authenticity of Dharma transmission is no guarantee against blind spots.

Nonetheless, the admonition that zazen is useless remains a very profound teaching, one that continually goes against the grain of all our self-centered expectations. Would we continue to "just sit" if we really believed nothing was going to happen as a result? And how do we react when nothing really does happen after years of sitting—when some problem or seemingly neurotic trait persists despite all those years of practice?

One of my favorite *New Yorker* cartoons shows a guru out playing golf with two young disciples. As he takes a mighty swing at the ball, one young monk whispers to the other, "If he's so enlightened, why can't he lick that slice?" This is a wonderful koan, one that echoes the dilemma posed by a traditional case from the *Wu-men Kuan*, "Wu-tsu's Buffalo Passes through the Window": "Its head, horns, and four legs all pass through. Why can't its little tail pass through as well?" Practice has taken us so far, so why can't we go all the way? But what is that supposed to mean? Where do you think practice should take us? To what perfect, problem-free sphere of existence should we be transported once and for all? What does it mean that imperfections remain after years of practice? Perhaps our cartoon guru has developed a fair measure of self-awareness and self-control in the face of frustration. His young disciples are probably right to expect that their guru will not angrily fling his clubs into the lake after he misses a shot, or be in a snit for the rest of the day over his bad score. But he still may be a lousy golfer.

We can laugh at the idea of remaining a lousy golfer despite all our best efforts, but what about something more serious, like being an alcoholic? That is a dilemma many teachers and sanghas have had to face. Here, "That's just who I am" is an unacceptable answer. It is in cases like this that psychoanalysis, with its understanding of unconscious processes and mechanisms of defense, helps us to discern the difference between self-acceptance and outright denial and enables us to take the necessary action. While unconscious patterns of thought remain, by definition, outside the thinker's conscious awareness, they are recognizable to an appropriately attuned observer. Everyone, no matter what level of mental health or spiritual maturity they think they have attained, should remain open to feedback from others regarding old patterns of self-centeredness that may have slipped under the radar of awareness.

And what about more ambiguous cases, like being in lousy health? Like so much of what we do, our health all too easily becomes a project. And that means we may end up endlessly judging how well or badly we're doing in our efforts. We fervently hold on to the hope that making the right effort will guarantee the right outcome. If only I eat all the right things, avoid all the bad ones, take the right combination of vitamins, do the right exercises, and so on, I'll stay healthy forever! Doubtless doing all that may make us healthier, but there are no guarantees. We may do all the right things, but the equivalent of that slice just won't go away. Sometimes we simply have no way of knowing what factors will lead to an unexpected illness, let alone accidents. Or the relevant factors, like a genetic heritage, may be completely out of our control. Both psychoanalysis and Buddhism have had adherents who believe that there is no such thing as an accident. Some classical analysts have held that hidden, guilt-ridden masochistic wishes lurk behind seemingly random accidents, and there are Buddhists who tell you everything happens according to a cosmic karmic calculus. Sometimes believing in determinism is more comforting than feeling at the mercy of pure chance.

With complex systems like our bodies, very minor changes may perturb the system in unforeseeable ways. The particular danger of overly deterministic thinking is that we interpret illnesses, when they inevitably occur, as failures, proof that we've done something wrong. We misconstrue the simple truth that stress can damage our health to mean that our every illness must have a hidden emotional conflict at its root. Then we suffer not only the illness itself but the self-hatred that accompanies our misguided sense of responsibility for our symptoms. Sadly, self-hatred is a price many seem willing to pay to keep alive a fantasy of perfection.

I'll give you an example from my own life. For a long time, I've had high blood pressure. I did what I thought were all the right things to stabilize it—altered diet, salt restriction, and the like—but none made much difference. At one point my wife introduced me to an elderly Chinese herbalist who prescribed various herbs. Maybe they helped a bit, maybe not. At one point the Chinese doctor suggested I try meditating. I explained that I had been meditating regularly for quite a few years. His immediate response was, "Then you're not meditating right!" So I asked him how I should meditate, and he said, "Sit quietly and empty the mind." Well, OK...

Now, I'm sure that for a lot of people, meditation does help control blood pressure. But of all the changes that practice has made in my life, that just hasn't been one of them—though I suppose you could always say that my blood pressure would have been worse without it. It simply seems in my case that this is something I'm prone to. Eventually, my internist gave me a pill to take, which has kept my blood pressure perfectly normal. I'm very grateful for that pill—even though some part of me would no doubt prefer to be able to say that through meditation or diet or some other virtuous habit, I had healed myself all on my own.

This issue comes up when I'm asked what I think of Zen students taking Prozac. Shouldn't practice all by itself quiet the mind and stabilize our moods? Isn't it another sign we're not doing something right if we need a drug like Prozac? As far as I'm concerned, practice is fundamentally about one thing: Are you living a self-centered life or a selfless life? And all those questions about whether I should be able to handle this on my own, what are they? Self-centered, of course! The real question ought to be "What allows me to function and respond best to those around me?" Everything else is a matter of pride and self-image.

The fact is, the deeper we allow practice to penetrate into our core beliefs and our fantasies of gain and ultimate perfectibility, the more our practice will disappoint us. Because at the deepest level neither practice nor life is going to be what we want them to be. As someone once said, there is no reason to believe that when we discover the truth it will turn out to be interesting. When we go looking for the truth, we all carry along some picture of what we want it to look like, but the truth isn't interested in our pictures!

I remember when I first started going out to San Diego in the mid-eighties to attend sesshins with Joko. I planned one trip with an old Zen friend with whom I had practiced in New York for many years. In most ways he was a far "better" Zen student than I was; he had attended many more sesshins over the years with different teachers, some very strict and demanding, and he was capable of great discipline and physical endurance. I've never been that tough. But he approached Zen the way somebody might take up mountain climbing: he exalted in the difficulty of it all and was exhilarated by the intensity of his efforts and his sense of mastering something that others thought impossible.

Anyway, we planned to go to San Diego together and were in the airport waiting for our flight, which kept getting delayed. And all of a sudden he got up and said, "You know, this isn't any fun!" And he walked out and went home. As far as I know that was the end of his Zen career. His core belief about practice had been brought right up to the surface; he wanted practice to be intense, difficult, exhilarating— something he could be proud to master. And all of a sudden, after all those years, and all those sesshins, it didn't feel anything like that. There was nothing heroic about being stuck overnight in the airport.

What we too often fail to recognize is that such moments of disappointment are the real fruits of our practice. Only when our illusory hopes and dreams of becoming who we want to be, or who think we should be, are crushed once and for all, are we ready genuinely to face who we are. We dread that moment more than anything else, but it is actually our moment of salvation. Hope dies, and shame and self-reproach die with it. This is not mere resignation. Resignation holds on to the idea that there really is something wrong with us that ought to be fixed, but we've given up hope that we'll ever be able to fix it. I'm talking about going a step further—realizing that the whole idea of fixing anything at all is simply and utterly impossible, even nonsensical. *This is it*. Period. Then, the whole crazy enterprise of self-hatred and self-improvement collapses like a house of cards.

Moments of intense disappointment are really our greatest opportunities. In those moments we are given the chance to set aside our old core beliefs about life and choose life as it is. But the truth when we see it may not be very "interesting," and we will be tempted to hold on to our fantasies, which may be much more heroic or romantic or tragic than this ordinary moment. The paradox is that the greatest rewards of practice come only when we allow ourselves to experience the greatest disappointments. Only then do we discover in ourselves a motivation that has nothing to do with getting or gaining.

One of the basic tenets of Buddhism has always been the inescapable fact of impermanence—and that means that fundamentally there will always be a limit to how much control we can exert over the way our lives go. There's no technique for attaining and holding on to some perfect, unchangeable state of mental or physical health, though it seems that everybody comes to practice with some fantasy of that sort. True practice entails letting go of that fantasy and learning to accept our life as it is, and ourselves as we are. We do what we can and deal with the limits of what we can do. We do not abdicate our responsibility to maintain a practice of life-long self-awareness; nor do we see practice as an endless treadmill of self-improvement.

Long after our so-called enlightenment, we may still slice our literal or metaphorical golf balls uncontrollably to the right, whether we dualistically label it as a problem or not. Many years of conditioning will remain to be worked through, and life will still contain difficulties. Neurosis doesn't evaporate into thin air. Our tendency to be frustrated or narcissistically injured will dramatically decrease when our practice reveals we have no essential self to defend. But if we imagine that our practice will lead us to a transcendent state in which we are totally impervious to the vicissitudes of life, we are falling into a trap—set perhaps by the glimpse of perfection we gained at our initial experience of kensho. At the end of the day, we are still ourselves, warts and all. After practicing for many years, receiving Dharma transmission, and serving as abbot of his temple, Uchiyama Roshi still admitted,

> In the middle of a solemn service, I am extremely self-conscious and so confused I make a big mess of it. Afterwards, I feel shame and remorse. But since my childhood, I have been so sensitive, that in self-defense, I ended up settling myself in the stability of "Whatever happens, I am I.".... Shy is shy. Careless is careless. There is nothing to do about it.... Even if we don't become refined and elegant, like an expert at *kendo* or like a master of *noh,* or of the tea ceremony, it doesn't matter, does it?

We will always remain embodied, mortal, living in a world of right and wrong, good and bad, life and death. That's where we live and where we need to function. As an analyst I see patients who believe there is something wrong with them; as a teacher I work with students striving to relieve their suffering. It certainly would be of no use to anyone if I were to announce right off the bat that right and wrong or happiness and suffering are just empty, dualistic delusions!

Dropping a dualistic and essentialist perspective doesn't take us out of this world; it allows us to move and function more freely in it. We can act more freely and effectively if we simply waste less time and energy trying to defend what isn't there in the first place and trying to fix what is perfect to begin with. After realization, we still practice—but not because we are endlessly working to eliminate the last vestiges of conditioning in our personalities. Our lives are perfect just as they are, and part of that perfection is our ongoing effort to make them better still.

"WASH YOUR BOWL"

The Case
*A monk said to Chao-chou, "I have just entered the monastery.
Please teach me."*
Chao-chou said, "Have you eaten your rice gruel?"
The monk said, "Yes, I have."
Chao-chou said, "Wash your bowl." The monk understood.

Wu-men's Comment
*Chao-chou opened his mouth and showed his gallbladder, his
heart, and his liver. I wonder if the monk really heard the truth.
I hope he did not mistake the bell for a jar.*

> *Because it's so very clear,*
> *it takes so long to realize.*
> *If you just know that flame is fire,*
> *you'll find your rice has long been cooked.*

When we come to practice what do we bring with us? When you
present yourself to a teacher what do you show?

Here we have the story of a monk who comes to Chao-chou
asking for instruction. Straightforward enough, you might say, but in
a way, a challenge to Chao-chou: "What do you have to offer me?"

Chao-chou turns the question back to the monk, "Have you
eaten your rice gruel?" A seemingly polite inquiry; the host is looking after his guest. But more subtly, Chao-chou might also be asking,

"What have you gotten so far? What kind of state are you in? Are you hungry or full?"

The monk replies, "Yes, I have." To say we're lacking something is to fall into one ditch; to say we've accomplished something is to fall into another. In this story the monk comes in with some sense of accomplishment. Nowadays, it is just as common for new students to come in and display their problems—what they think is wrong with them, what they think they're lacking, and what they think Zen will provide. They stretch out their bowls and beg, "Feed me!"

Chao-chou says, "Wash your bowl." Whatever you've brought with you, whatever you think you've accomplished—wash it away.

But here's the interesting part: *How* do you wash it away? How do you clean your metaphorical mental bowl of whatever it is you're carrying around? And the answer is, Wash your *real* bowl—not the one up in your head, but the one that's right here in your hands. Wholeheartedly engage with this moment's activity and everything else disappears—your bowl is spotless. In traditional Zen language we might call this washing your bowl without using your hands.

Just be this moment. Wu-men says that Chao-chou spills his guts—he shows everything that there is to be shown. Just this. How simple. But, as his verse says, because it's so simple, "so very clear, / it takes so long to realize." When we see that this moment is all there is—when we realize that "flame is fire" (what could be more obvious?), we find that our "rice has long been cooked"—everything we need we already have.

As I say, all that sounds simple enough: just be this moment. But, of course, that's easier said than done—"it takes so long to realize." We wash our bowls in the present moment, but some of the gunk in there is pretty sticky.... We may need some scouring powder. The way we practice here, the kind of scouring powder we use, is our awareness of resistance and difficulty. What intrudes on our wholehearted functioning in the moment? Expectation. Hope.

Disappointment. How do we recognize them? By the hallmarks of resistance: our anger, our fear, our anxiety.

Once, during an April Fool's Day sesshin we served hot dogs, potato chips, and Diet Pepsi for lunch. That meal stuck to a few bowls! And so we had to scour away our attachments to purity, to specialness, to always having what's wholesome and proper. Sometimes we just have to take what life serves up and watch our reaction.

It's how we use the experience of difficulty that allows us to scour the really persistent attachments that cling to the surface of our bowls. This is where the practices of Zen and psychotherapy dovetail. Zen says, "Be just this moment." Therapy says, "Look at all the expectations, all the hope and dread that you habitually bring to this moment. Where did *they* come from?" We experience difficulty when our old expectations of ourselves or of others get frustrated in some way or another. Practice means not only bringing ourselves back to a pure awareness and attention of this moment but also acknowledging that this moment includes all of what we've brought to it. In the language of this koan, we acknowledge all that we've eaten (and not fully digested!) before showing up for a first interview with the teacher.

This is the real work of practice: Having seen clearly what clings to our bowls, we wash them clean *by* washing them clean, and by drying, stacking, and putting them away—by being the activity of each moment just as it is.

CHAPTER ELEVEN

RELATIONSHIP
AND AUTHORITY

W HAT IS THE RELATIONSHIP of a student to a Zen teacher? Is it analogous to that of a patient and a psychoanalyst? How central is this relationship to what happens in meditation?

I have had psychoanalytic colleagues who, prizing the intimacy, mutuality, and relatedness they achieve over the years with their patients, assure me that the Zen student/teacher relationship must inevitably be distorted by issues of hierarchy and authority. They ask, "What kind of freedom could anyone possibly find within such a rigidly formalized, hierarchical relationship?" Yet anyone who has had a long-standing student-teacher relationship can testify to the level of intimacy that is achieved. Superficially, of course, a Zen teacher takes a very different stance toward a student than an analyst toward a patient. The analyst's basic stance is one of engaged, personal inquiry; the Zen teacher's is one of challenge, if only the challenge of leaving everything alone. I've often joked that the quintessential analytic intervention is a curious and quizzical *Really?*, while the Zen teacher's quintessential response is *So what!* The analyst actively explores the subjective meaning of each moment's experience; the Zen teacher emphasizes the uniqueness of each moment, stripping it of all past associations and conceptualizations.

Many who have had the terrible experience of having someone else's version of reality imposed on them will fear renewed trauma if they submit to any authority, whether spiritual or therapeutic. The potential for new injury is just as real in analysis as in any religious practice. One hallmark of an intersubjectively attuned stance is that it actively explores the way current impasses and conflicts are co-created by both participants, and are not simply the result of the patient's transferential distortions. Psychoanalysts are trained to stay attuned to this danger of re-traumatization and to be mindful of the ways an analyst may inadvertently recreate old patterns of pathological accommodation and compliance. And yet it is only a new experience of authority and expertise, one exercised in a non-traumatizing, validating manner that can redeem authority and discipline for those previously traumatized by its misuse. Any attempt at an artificially contrived mutuality—one that in effect denies the latent differences in authority and power inherent in a professional or student/teacher relationship—tacitly reinforces the patient's or student's mistrust of all authority or hierarchy. When they deny authority, hierarchy, or expertise, both analysts and teachers implicitly send the message that these things are intrinsically untrustworthy or are aspects of their roles that they are uncomfortable in acknowledging and wielding.

Ideally, the Zen teacher exercises a non–self-centered authority, an authority of skillful means, responsive to the particular needs and defenses of the individual student. What does that look like? There can be no one answer to that question, because just as there are wide differences between analysts and schools of analysis, there is no single style that characterizes all Zen teachers or how they operate.

According to some popular characterizations, the Zen teacher is a master of paradox who uses koans to drive the student into a conceptual impasse, from which to break through into a wholly new, nonconceptual, nondualistic way of being. For some Zen teachers, no doubt, extreme austerity and strictness were the guarantors of authentic insight. Perhaps we can draw an analogy with the classical Freudian insistence on a pure analytic neutrality and abstinence as the guarantors of the transference neurosis. A "real" analyst never spoke except to offer an interpretation, let alone give advice or reassurance. In Zen, the strictest teachers were the ones who were called "grandmotherly," since they compassionately offered their students the most direct experience of the Way, as if they were offering a lychee already peeled and ready to swallow. One such grandmotherly teacher, Luzu, is said to have responded to all his students' questions by turning his back to them and silently facing the wall.

But contrast this way of teaching with the following description of Soto teacher Shunryu Suzuki's style. A new student who had been intending to go to Japan to study Zen came to the zendo saying that

> he'd read some books about Zen and enlightenment and now he wanted to meet the real thing....Suzuki told him...it might be good to have some experience with Zen practice in America first. He got a cushion from the altar, placed it in the aisle, and showed [him] how to sit. He corrected his posture, pushing the small of his back in, pulling his shoulders back and his chin in. He pushed his knees down gently, showing him how to put his hands together with the left palm on the right palm and the thumbs touching just enough to hold a piece of paper between them. He told him to keep his eyes half open, and to place his attention on the in and out of his breath. He advised him in the future to wear looser pants, so his legs would cross more easily....This was not at all what [the new student] expected. The books on Zen were full of dramatic interchanges between monks.

> But there was something about this priest that made
> him want to return. Beneath the charm [he] sensed
> authority and humility.

This is a teaching that challenges not by paradox but by its very simplicity. If there's any paradox, it is that we cannot believe that the answers to all our questions are so simple. What wisdom does the great Zen master offer his new student? Wear looser pants!

Expecting the extraordinary, we are surprised by the ordinary. Just sitting. Sitting itself is the answer. We are so sure that Zen is something extraordinary that we are surprised when it turns out to be so ordinary. Just sit. And yet, who can manage to obey that simple injunction?

Here's what my own teacher, Joko Beck, wrote about the authority of the teacher:

> The last words of the Buddha were, "Be a lamp unto
> yourself." He didn't say, "Go running to this teacher
> or that teacher, to this center or that center"—he said,
> "Look—be a lamp unto yourself." …There is only
> one teacher. What is that teacher? Life itself…. Now
> life happens to be both a severe and endlessly kind
> teacher. It's the only authority that you need to trust.
> And this teacher, this authority, is everywhere.

How can we come to terms with the paradox inherent in a Zen teacher *telling* us, "Be a lamp unto yourself"? Isn't such an admonition as useless as "Be spontaneous"? The tension that must be resolved here is actually between the tendency to believe that *either* there is someone with all the answers to whom I will defer as my teacher *or* I must be my own authority. Whether in Zen or in analysis, we can spend years ricocheting between "I can't live without you" and "I don't need anybody to tell *me* what to do!" Paradoxically, we need the structure of practice and the ongoing presence of a teacher precisely to break through this false dichotomy. And when it collapses, life becomes our teacher. Buddha's exhortation "Be a lamp unto yourself" does not mean you should become preoccupied with the light of your own self-experience (especially your enlightenment experience). He means we should use our realization to illuminate the life around us. Seeing and responding to our life is what real practice and real therapy is all about. We are ready to go out on our own, not when we're finally once and for all "enlightened" or "cured," but when self-awareness and self-acceptance have replaced self-improvement as the core of our practice and our life.

Once when I was ending a visit to Joko, I suddenly found myself aware of her advancing years, and it occurred to me that any time with her might be my last. Becoming tearful, I said, "I may never see you again." She responded, "I don't care if I ever see you again. That you know how to practice is what's important." This brought me up short, but it has proved truer and truer to me over the years. When my wife Deborah was killed in a plane crash, I called Joko and simply thanked her for giving me the resources to go through the pain of that terrible loss. More and more, when someone asked me what Joko would say about something, I simply started talking about it myself— there seemed no boundary between my sense of practice and hers. That is true intimacy, and life itself is the true teacher that never leaves.

EMPATHY

Now I want to address more specifically the impact of Zen training on my analytic practice. People often ask me what it means to be a Zen psychoanalyst, or they inquire whether my analytic stance has been fundamentally altered by my Zen training. In fact, working as

I do from a background in self psychology, I believe the basic analytic stance of empathic inquiry needs little direct input from Zen. Empathy by definition is a non–self-centered stance. As Yamada Koun Roshi has said, "Zen practice is a matter of forgetting the self in the act of uniting with something." Substitute "uniting with *someone*" and you have Zen and the art of empathy. One necessarily suspends one's own world-view (as best as one can) and endeavors to see life through the eyes of the patient, immersing oneself in the subjectivity of the other. The patient's subjective experience of *feeling understood* is the one necessary and sufficient criterion for judging how empathic we are. Incidents of misunderstanding are clear enough signs of my self-centeredness intruding. I do believe I have a greater capacity to sit and stay with another person's emotional experience as a result of my Zen practice. But there is little in my basic analytic stance that I've consciously altered because of Zen. For me, empathy remains a far more reliable and less self-centered approach than one that keeps its focus on the analyst's state of mind, even one emphasizing the analyst's commitment to openness.

Some psychoanalysts like Michael Eigen, the author of *The Psychoanalytic Mystic*, have tried to incorporate what they see as a Zen-like "not knowing" into their basic analytic stance. Eigen sees himself following the lead of the British psychoanalyst W. R. Bion, who contrasted what he called, in his own idiosyncratic idiom, the state of "O" (unknowing or the unknowable) with the analyst's usual stance of "K" (focusing on knowledge or insight). This reification of "not knowing" runs the risk, I'm afraid, of placing the analyst's own purity of mind ahead of the patient's simple desire to feel understood. Echoing the old Chinese master, Nan-ch'üan, I'd say to them, "Forget about the Unknowable, your ordinary mind is the way." What is this ordinary mind? Simply a mind unentangled in the isolated mind's dualistic fantasies of delusion and enlightenment, a mind that has forgotten about its own condition.

Although my empathy-based psychoanalytic stance has not been much altered by my Zen practice, my attitudes regarding mental "illness" and what it means to suggest medication or therapy for someone's problems have dramatically changed due to my overall Buddhist perspective. I routinely ask prospective patients whether they have any experience with meditation, yoga, or the martial arts in much the same way I routinely inquire whether they have previously been in therapy or have taken drugs or medication to cope with their distress. Often patients who initially come for a consultation about whether they should take Prozac or some other psychotropic medication are eager to discuss alternate means of stabilizing their moods.

As I've said, I have no problem with my patients or students taking Prozac. But one of the more pervasive, and I think pernicious, notions surrounding the use of Prozac and other such drugs is the idea that if someone who takes them gets relief from their depression, then that proves that their depression was "really" biologically based all along. At the same time they assume, just as erroneously, that if a depression can be cured by psychotherapy or some other practice like meditation, it must have been "merely" psychological in its origins.

From a Buddhist perspective there are a number of things obviously wrong with this way of thinking. First and foremost, there is the dualistic split between mind and body, and the assumption that a symptom must be either biological or psychological in origin. It is no solution to this fundamentally dualistic way of thinking to say instead that a symptom like depression arises out of a combination of biological and interpersonal factors. Instead we have to recognize that we are dealing with constantly changing complex systems (i.e., displaying dependent co-origination) for which no linear explanation is appropriate.

An interesting analogy can be made between such complex systems as minds and the recursive functions that Benoit Mandelbrot described as giving rise to fractal geometries. Recursive functions are simple mathematical feedback systems, wherein for a given function f, where $f(x) = y$, the value derived for y is fed back as the next x on which the function operates. When the succession of x's and y's was plotted graphically, Mandelbrot discovered that extremely complex patterns could be generated from very simple recursive functions. Interestingly, very small differences in the initial value of x led to elaborately different patterns—suggestive of the way simple invariant organizing principles or core beliefs (e.g., "I can't trust anyone"), given different interpersonal contexts, can result in widely differing individual stances and strategies of coping. For instance, a core belief in other people's untrustworthiness can be elaborated in a variety of distinct personality styles. For the avoidant personality, distrust leads to defensive isolation; in the borderline personality, distrust manifests as hypervigilance and a tendency to be easily offended and angered. For narcissistic individuals, basic distrust can take the form of an arrogant self-assertion that denies the worth or contribution of others.

When we're dealing with complex living systems, there is never any single beginning to the recursive sequence, no single event that can be pointed to as *the cause*. Furthermore, we must always make a choice about what *level of description* is most relevant for any given state of the system. Problems that are intractable at one level of description may prove to be conceptually simpler or more manageable at another. Right now it's easier to prescribe a serotonin re-uptake inhibitor like Prozac than to attempt to alter the genetic sequence controlling serotonin production. The danger is that we identify the "cause" of a problem solely on the basis of the level at which we find it most convenient to make an intervention. The meditator whose depression is relieved by zazen can say nothing about what "caused" his depression any more than the Prozac patient can. What can be used to stabilize a system tells us *nothing at all* about what perturbed the system in the first place. Imagine a clay pot wobbling as it takes shape on a potter's wheel. We can dampen the wobble and stabilize its spin by gently placing our hands on opposite sides of the pot. But *where* on the pot we place our hands makes no difference and has nothing to do with whatever imbalance started the pot wobbling in the first place.

When analyzing a problem or "symptom" in a complex system, there is no absolute basis for preferring or privileging one level of description over another. Everything can be described in terms of subatomic quarks, if you wish, but that's the wrong level at which to try to fix a flat tire, analyze a poem, or play baseball.

I like to use the game of baseball to illustrate some aspects of interdependency and the fluidity of boundaries—like the boundaries of the self—whose permanence or fixity we normally take for granted. What do we need to have for a game of baseball? Well, we can start with a bat and ball, fielders' gloves and, of course, two teams of players. Maybe the teams will need coaches as well. We need a field that is properly laid out with the proper distances between the bases and the pitcher's mound and home plate. The grounds need to be maintained and the grass mowed, so maybe we need a grounds crew too. If we're going to have professional teams, we will need owners, investors, accountants, and a league commissioner. And what about transportation to the stadium, and someone to sell hot dogs and beer? Who will sing the national anthem?

By now, surely you're ready to protest that I'm adding on too much. If you ever played sandlot ball as a kid, you know you can vary just about every aspect of the field and number of players and all sorts of other things and still have a game called "baseball." What I'm pointing to is that there is no nonarbitrary, clear boundary to what is included when we talk about baseball—just as there can be no clear boundary to what we call the "self." The game—or the self—is ultimately inseparable from its surround. And when there is a difficulty—like the team is having a losing season—the level at which we intervene to turn the team around may be quite arbitrary, even though when something makes a difference we may think we've identified and fixed the "cause" of the problem. Do we trade unproductive players? or hire new coaches to motivate the team or hone their skills? Either might work. Maybe moving the team to another city where the other teams in the division are less talented would make for a better season, although not necessarily a trip to the World Series. A new owner might infuse the team with more cash to pursue free agents. Any of these interventions—affecting players, coaches, locations, or money—might make a difference in the team's statistics. But the level of intervention doesn't prove anything about what was "wrong" in the first place. All it shows is that the system could be altered in a number of different ways.

I think you can see how this would apply to the concept of mental illness. For one thing, I am no longer inclined to think of anyone's problem as having a single, diagnosable cause located "inside" of them. Particular problems arise in particular contexts. It is important to investigate what contexts foster their emergence or disappearance. So ultimately there can be no clear distinction between therapies that are psychoanalytic (looking into one's subjective experience or personal history) and those that are behavioral (reinforcing or diminishing current behaviors or symptoms without regard to their origins); those that are systems oriented (looking "outside" to family or group dynamics) or ones that are biologically based (offering genetic and biochemical explanations). There is no one way to deal with human suffering any more than there can be any one description of the problem.

Both Zen practice and psychoanalysis challenge us to become aware of the complex systems that constitute our core beliefs and our patterns of relating. These patterns come vividly to life as we respond in our own characteristic fashion to the teacher and the analyst. Our inner distress will be reflected in our outer modes of attachment, expectation, and defensiveness. With luck, and with a good teacher or a good analyst, the old systems are perturbed just enough to destabilize our old reflexive ways of thinking and behaving, and new patterns can then emerge, centered on a wholly new view of self, other, and world.

ATTACHMENT AND DETACHMENT

I'd like to discuss how attachment and detachment are commonly understood—and misunderstood—in Western psychology and in Buddhism. We find attachment and detachment referred to in both therapeutic and spiritual contexts, but with very different meanings. In Western psychology, attachment means relatedness, the ability to form intimate, loving relationships. Authentic relatedness, or mature attachment, is difficult to achieve. Our self-involvement, narcissistic vulnerabilities, and various inner conflicts all lead us to form unhealthy, neurotic attachments. We form an attachment to someone to meet what we think are our needs and to relieve our particular anxieties, rather than relating to this other person as another whole individual on a basis of mutuality and respect. Detachment in this psychological schema refers to an individual's *giving up* on attachment because of an inability to face the vulnerabilities or conflicts that relationships inevitably entail. The detached person tries to become autonomous and self-sufficient, and to hold on to some inner peace of mind by avoiding entangling relationships. Often these individuals prefer aesthetic, philosophical, and religious feelings to the more ordinary and uncontrollable emotions of interpersonal attachments.

Buddhism has nothing against the positive qualities of mature attachment in this sense, but here the concept of attachment has traditionally referred to neurotic clinging and those attempts to control one's inner and outer environment that inevitably backfire and lead to suffering. And Buddhism certainly has recognized the dangers involved in the pathological varieties of detachment. There's an old story that illustrates this point:

Once, an old woman, as an act of charity, undertook to support a monk living in a nearby hermitage. The monk was an austere and seemingly holy fellow who needed very little in the way of food, clothing, or shelter. But after a couple of years the old woman decided to test the monk. She sent her beautiful daughter out to the hermitage and instructed her to put her arms around his neck and ask, "Mr. Monk, do you think I'm beautiful?" Well, the monk just sat there impassively, and after a moment said, "A withered tree doesn't notice the change of seasons." So the beautiful daughter went back to her mother and told her what the monk had said. Whereupon the old lady went out and burned down his hermitage and drove him away, yelling, "I can't believe I've wasted all my hard-earned money on a fraud like you!"

The old woman in the story recognized that the monk was detached in the neurotic sense, trying to avoid all feeling, and to retreat into some unchanging state he thought of as pure.

The proper, positive meaning of detachment in Buddhism instead centers on an awareness of impermanence. Suzuki Roshi once said that detachment doesn't mean giving up the things of the world, but accepting that they go away. What we "detach" from is not other people or our emotions but rather our neurotic, self-centered attempt to make things and relationships permanent or to have them be just the way we want for our own selfish motives.

Another common mistake is to think that detachment means we should always just passively accept what's happening. If we're living in a apartment with terrible noisy neighbors, out-of-control teenagers, barking dogs, and so on, how should we practice detachment? Does being a good Zen student mean saying to ourselves,

"Well, I guess I really shouldn't be attached to being able to sleep at night, or to having enough peace and quiet to study"? That isn't spiritual practice, that's just masochism! Detachment means non-–self-centered responsiveness to a situation. Sometimes that will mean enduring unavoidable suffering and acknowledging that life is not under our control. But it also means taking appropriate action—talking to the neighbors, calling the landlord, and, if it comes to that, moving! All detachment precludes is increasing the suffering of others in order to minimize your own. Detachment in the proper sense means working through our selfishness so that we can act compassionately. Then we form the genuine mature attachments that Western psychology so rightly values.

CHAPTER TWELVE

ONE PRACTICE
OR TWO?

In the days before I received permission from my Zen teacher to begin teaching and to open the Ordinary Mind Zendo, many of my patients nonetheless were aware that I had been practicing Zen. Indeed some had initially sought me out as their analyst because they wanted someone who could understand their own spiritual practices. Many other patients, however, came to me knowing nothing about Zen, referred by an insurance company or by a colleague or friend and sometimes, as I've said, just wanting to ask about Prozac.

These days, though, more and more of my patients who come for therapy at least once a week begin adding one or more meditation sessions in the zendo (and often a daily sitting practice at home) to their therapy routine, and some of them eventually sign up for a sesshin. By and large, the transitions from couch to cushion and back again have gone smoothly, reflecting, I believe, a perception by all concerned that what happens in the two settings are, in fact, aspects of a single practice. Whether through the vehicle of empathic inquiry or through just sitting, the goal of experiencing life as it is—including all the split-off affects accumulated by a lifetime of trying to *avoid* life as it is—remains constant.

Yet every patient's and every student's experience remains uniquely his or her own. What makes integrating these two modes of practice work is a willingness on my part to let everyone integrate them in their own individual way. For some, the two approaches address the same set of issues; for others, the practices focus on what feels like very different aspects of the self. One man, who originally came to me for treatment of depression, found that all the same transferential issues that arose in his therapy followed him into the zendo: fears of disappointing me, of being a failure, of not getting what others got from therapy or sitting. Another woman spoke of needing years of therapy simply to talk about herself, to trust someone to listen to and understand all that she had gone through and struggled with. Only then was she able to experience zazen as a practice not so much, in her words, "about myself" or some "problem" as about just being open to one thing after another.

Others' reactions have centered on what it has been like to go from individual therapy to practicing with a group. For one woman, the transition meant a painful loss of my exclusive attention, and a constant preoccupation with my relationship with the other group members. Another person, having grown used to my sensitivity to her fragile sense of vulnerability during years of analysis, had a hard time with the seemingly brusque way fellow students wielded authority as zendo monitors. Many others have welcomed the chance to practice within a group and have found it an engaging and enlivening alternative to solitary sitting. One young man delighted in being given responsibility to be the chant leader; the chance to prove himself in this way had been all too lacking within his family and in a succession of menial jobs. For others, taking on any public role, whether ringing the gong, serving meals, or leading chants, was fraught with anxiety. Having to perform in public made immediate and visible issues that were only alluded to in individual therapy. Not much liking public speaking myself, I encourage each person going through the Jukai ceremony (in which one receives the moral and ethical precepts) to give a brief talk to the group about one of the precepts they've studied. For Zen students, embarrassment is often harder to face than physical pain.

The way in which my students and patients view me reflects a striking range of attitudes and perceptions. For some, I'm clearly the same person in both the office and the zendo and the difference in my roles hardly registers. For others, each role remains distinct, and the way we communicate in daisan feels completely different from the way we talk in therapy. One man who began therapy and Zen practice at the same time (after years of practice within a different Buddhist tradition) said I struck him as more open, informal, more "street" in therapy, where I showed up "without the artifice of zendo and Buddhism." Yet another woman, who began sitting with the group after years of individual psychoanalytic therapy, remarked that she felt that I was now both her teacher and her friend, and that she knew me in all sorts of ways (and knew all sorts of things about me!) that never were possible within the confines of the traditional analyst/patient relationship.

While many of my analytic patients eventually want to find out about Zen practice or receive some beginning instruction in sitting, I am careful to ensure that they not feel pressured in any way to take up meditation. I am actually quite pleased when a patient with no particular background in spiritual practice gives sitting a try but then freely tells me that Zen is definitely not for them! If analytic neutrality still means anything at all, it has to mean not having any particular agenda for the patient—no particular picture of how things ought to proceed or what the outcome should be. I have tried to be very careful about not creating a group of "second-class citizens"—patients who for one reason or another don't want to follow me into the zendo. Nor do I try to prejudge who will likely benefit from Zen and who shouldn't try it. The example of the late Issan

Dorsey, a once drug-addled drag queen who eventually became the Dharma successor to Richard Baker at the San Francisco Zen Center and who ran their AIDS hospice program for many years before his own death from that disease, should give us all pause before we too quickly make a pronouncement on who is likely to be able to withstand and benefit from the rigors of Zen practice.

In the same way, I am very cautious about recommending therapy to anyone who comes to study with me in the zendo; that suggestion should always come from the student. No Zen student is ever subtly pressured into becoming an analytic patient anymore than any patient is pressured to study Zen. This should be obvious, but I find I must remain very alert lest I unconsciously lead someone to feel I expect some such thing from them. My analyst colleagues have, over the years, rightly raised questions about the difficulty involved in keeping my balance around this issue. It's one that will always remain a concern, and I am all too aware that some students will feel or fear that compliance with some latent Buddhist or therapeutic agenda of mine is the precondition of our relationship.

BOUNDARIES

Some colleagues have also raised the question as to whether serving simultaneously as someone's Zen teacher and their analyst does not in and of itself constitute a violation of professional boundaries. This question of boundaries is an important one, but we must try to be very clear what the terms of the question mean. What exactly is supposed to be kept within boundaries and what function does that serve? What exactly is "out of bounds"?

One traditional way of talking about boundaries held that analysts should keep a clear boundary between their personal and professional lives. This use of boundaries precluded the analyst not only from engaging in a personal relationship with the patient out-side of the treatment hour but also from allowing his own personal life, his opinions or emotional reactions, to intrude upon the ana-lytic relationship. The function of these prohibitions was twofold: first and foremost, that the patient should not be used to gratify the analyst's own emotional needs—sexual or otherwise. Second, facts about the analyst's "real" life (for instance whether straight or gay, married or single, and so on) should not be so intrusive in the ther-apy that the patient is unable to freely develop whatever fantasies might emerge in the course of the transference. For instance, one patient of mine (who showed no interest in Zen) remarked how her previous therapy had been marred by the fact that her therapist was also her neighbor in the small town where she lived. She regularly encountered her therapist in shops, restaurants, at the gym, or at the beach. She found her own worries about the therapist's life intrusive and that her knowledge of his personal problems (including mari-tal problems) made it hard for her to envision him as the stable, reliable parental figure she longed to have in her life.

A classically trained Freudian analyst would traditionally attempt to prevent this sort of contamination of the transference not only by carefully avoiding all personal contacts with a patient outside of the analytic hour, but by maintaining silence, neutrality, and anonymity within the session as well. However, more and more contemporary analysts are coming to the conclusion that perfect anonymity and neutrality are both questionable as ideals and, in any case, unattainable in practice. Our race, patterns of speech, gen-der, style of dressing, office decoration and location all inevitably speak volumes about who we are. Our goal as analysts, therefore, must be not to strive to eliminate the impact of these inevitable latent communications, but to acknowledge their existence and strive to make explicit their impact on our patients' perceptions and fantasies. An intersubjective approach assumes that the analyst's personality, her actions and inactions, always and continually shape the course of the treatment. Like many other contemporary analysts, I now employ a stance that stresses *emotional availability* rather than neutrality. Donna Orange, the analyst who coined that phrase, put it this way,

> Embracing the concept of emotional availability erases neutrality and anonymity as rules for analytic conduct. Analysts who are emotionally available adjust how much they reveal of themselves to their patients, in the same way parents attune their level of availability to the child.

As parents know all too well, any strict boundaries we try to set up will often end up being far more permeable than we'd like to imagine. I have found that the best way to deal with the subtle issue of the boundary between my analytic and Zen practices is not by trying to make that boundary rigid but rather by staying attuned to its fluidity and the impact my dual roles may be having with each individual patient or student.

It has been a basic premise of this book, and of my teaching and analytic practices that, in fact, no sharp conceptual boundary can be drawn between the psychological and the spiritual. Systems of practice to explore the nature of self and of suffering evolved independently in the East and West, and these two systems are now involved in a process of cross-fertilization. The Buddha's discovery of the emptiness of the self and the interconnectedness of all beings promoted a unified picture of psychology and spirituality in the East. In the West, the two understandings of psychology and spirituality developed largely along separate tracks and are only now beginning to reconnect.

In the preceding chapters, my primary goal has been to translate the language of one practice into the language of the other in order to foster mutual understanding. My project is in no way an attempt to write a "how-to" manual for meditation teachers who want to practice therapy or for therapists who want to act like Zen masters. A little knowledge, as the saying goes, can be a dangerous thing.

My own position—having spent decades training and becoming certified in both the practice of psychoanalysis and Zen is, for now at least, highly unusual—though no doubt destined to become less so in the years to come. Combining the two practices has evolved naturally and—so far—effectively in my life and in the lives of my students and patients. Most of the time I am able to move from one role to another in a way analogous to the way therapists do when they see clients both in individual and group therapy. A therapist will no doubt behave and be perceived differently in those two settings, but the basic premises of therapy and the underlying expectations of professionalism on the part of the therapist remain constant. Issues will arise in one modality that may remain in the background in the other, and many clients will benefit from the dual perspective, though there will be some who progress better if they work in only one mode. Just as many analysts by temperament or training confine themselves to a single modality of therapy, so we can anticipate that there will be a wide variation in the extent to which future generations of therapist–Zen teachers will integrate or keep separate these two modes of practice.

There is by now a whole body of literature on the potential synergies (and difficulties) of combining individual and group therapy. Because these two therapies are seen as essentially a single practice conducted on two different fronts, the question of boundary violations does not arise, and the therapist's choice to employ one or the other, or both, is strategic rather than ethical. But no such perception of a common ground exists regarding psychoanalysis and, say, economics, and thus one would rightly be suspicious of a therapist who offered to analyze both your dreams and your retirement port-folio. Exploring and defining the common ground of therapy and Zen meditation is clearly still an experiment-in-progress, and only many more years of collective experience will reveal its full advantages and disadvantages.

My hope is that therapists will gradually begin to absorb from Zen the awareness that sometimes the most profound transformations occur precisely when we stop trying to change, fix, or improve our lives. Likewise, I hope Zen teachers will gradually become more attuned to the transference and counter-transference reactions that inevitably arise in student-teacher relationships; transference occurs whether you call what you're doing therapy or not! Both the student and teacher are ill-served by a mindset that denies—or worse, stigmatizes—the inevitable occurrences of transference.

One prominent Zen teacher, in a recent revealing interview, admitted how his own tendency to strictly compartmentalize the psychological and the spiritual contributed to his indulging in sexual relationships with his students that led to his eventual ousting from the Zen center over which he presided. This Zen teacher says the following:

> [W]hile I was well aware of the dictum that psycho-analysts not have sexual relationships with their patients, I did not think that the relationship between a Zen teacher and a practitioner was in any way similar. I saw Zen students as strong, not as weak, and not as patients.

Basic ethical guidelines can, of course, provide communities and individuals with some safeguards, but ultimately I believe that the origin of the most serious problems that arise from so-called boundary violations are the result of personal shortcomings, not structural ones. Unresolved narcissistic needs of analysts and teachers are, I believe, almost always at the root of those boundary violations in which teachers have had sexual relationships with their students or patients. No matter how rigidly we try to legislate or codify professional boundaries, whether a teacher or analyst acts appropriately will always come down to how ethically or unethically that individual is willing and able to behave in any given instance. In the end, it is the unexamined character flaws in the analyst or teacher—not the form the practice takes—that generate harm.

It is interesting to note that, for better or worse, Freud himself was not always a strict "Freudian" in the sense that, contrary to his stringent rules for his followers, he allowed himself a great deal of technical leeway with his own patients. He would give advice or suggestions (telling one patient, "You must go to medical school!"), discuss one patient with another, and even went so far as to analyze his own daughter. The danger, of course, is that the Master (whether Doctor Freud or Roshi Such-and-Such) comes to believe that his own rules simply do not apply to him. When this happens, then what starts out as technical leeway or an exercise in what one imagines to be skillful means becomes a rationale for all sorts of egocentrically motivated behavior and even abuse. In such cases, the teacher's or analyst's unexamined motives must be explicitly brought to the surface and addressed in an appropriate modality. Neither a teacher nor a therapist should ever be allowed to remain on a pedestal, totally beyond criticism or feedback. This was what happened with the first generation of American Zen teachers; because "Enlightenment" was so novel and teachers so rare, no one knew what to expect from a teacher or where and when (if ever) to draw a line with regard to questionable behaviors.

This problem was compounded in monastic and community settings where not only was the roshi one's spiritual advisor, but he determined your job, where you lived, and perhaps even whether your kids had health insurance. Michael Downing has chronicled the unfolding of just such a dilemma in his history of the San Francisco Zen Center. As one student told him, "As [Dharma] heir and Abbot, [the roshi] was the ultimate authority on everything.... He was involved in every detail of my life." Another one of Downing's interviewees surmised that many of the Zen center's problems arose because "[The roshi] had reached the point where he isn't getting any feedback about how he looks or what he's doing." No set of rules or guidelines will, in and of themselves, suffice to keep in check the unexamined personality problems of a teacher. But checks and balances do help things from getting out of hand. Following this all-too-powerful roshi's resignation, the community decided to impose term limits on their abbots and democratize the community's decision-making process, turning more and more responsibility over to a board of elders.

To the extent that fuzzy role-definition can be the source of boundary problems, the sort of unchecked authority that the San Francisco Zen Center's early organization represents creates far more dangerous problems than the ones likely to be generated by the skillful practice of both meditation and therapy.

Nonetheless, it pays to be vigilant. There is much to be said for maintaining the checks and balances inherent in keeping the two practices separate. One very real advantage is that each can keep an eye on the other! Students and patients may both be all too inclined to accept inappropriate behaviors from their therapists and teachers simply believing that that is what therapy or Zen practice is, or out of a compliant fear of disrupting an all-important relationship. And yet, I have found in my own work that it is possible to combine the two, guided by empathy and a careful eye on the impact each practice is having on the other in the cases of each individual. In my own case, I think a further safeguard exists in the fact that our sangha includes people in all sorts of different relations to me:

patients, former patients, individuals in therapy with different therapists, and students in no therapy at all. The multiplicity of views this generates helps keep me from assuming a single authoritative role in everyone's eyes.

THE COUCH AND THE CUSHION

One thing about my analytic practice that has changed over the years has been my use of the couch. Traditionally, along with having at least three sessions a week, having the patient lie down on the couch was thought of as one of the hallmarks that distinguished a true psychoanalysis from "mere" psychotherapy. That distinction seems to make less and less difference to me these days. I now would say that analysis is characterized more by the nature of the relationship of patient to analyst, the mode of inquiry employed, by the intensity of the transference and the level of interpretation, and by the patient's willingness to begin an open-ended process of self-exploration. All of these factors can be present in a once-a-week treatment, or absent from one taking place four times a week.

For those patients who have come to sit with me in the zendo, facing the wall has largely replaced their use of the analytic couch. Traditionally, lying on the couch was thought to facilitate a therapeutic regression—a state of increased vulnerability in which one's childhood longings and frustrations would be allowed to come to the fore in the analytic relationship. Deprived of the ordinary social cues and responses from the analyst, the patient was allowed—and, in fact, sometimes felt forced—to turn inward, and to let long-suppressed fantasies and wishes come to light. In fact, much the same thing occurs for meditators who sit facing a blank wall. To face the wall is to face oneself.

Often both experiences can be disorienting or frightening until a stable, secure sense of the process and of others (both the teacher and fellow sangha members) is established. Either practice is useful only so long as a person can maintain a basic trust in what is going on. Fragile individuals who feel disconnected and cut off do better in face-to-face therapy until they establish a firmer sense of self and other. Prematurely being told to lie down on a couch or to sit and silently face the wall is a poor prescription for someone who has spent a lifetime feeling ignored, misunderstood, and isolated. A warm, empathic, responsive connection is usually a better first step. Even prior to opening the zendo, I rarely suggested using the couch at the very beginning of treatment. My usual practice was to wait and see how our relationship developed. I find it hard to get to know someone if, from the very start, I'm only talking to the top of their head! But I keep the couch as an option for nonmeditators looking for a traditional in-depth analytic experience.

And it is a very comfortable spot for my afternoon nap.

WHAT SHAKES YOUR TREE?

Once there was a monk who lived in an old temple, taking care of his retired teacher and tending the temple's famous garden. One day, visitors were coming from far away to admire the garden, and so he spent the morning meticulously raking the sand and carefully gathering up all the stray leaves. After he had gotten everything to look just right, he noticed his old master looking over the garden wall at his work. "Very nice," the old man said, "but there's one thing missing." "What's that?" asked the monk. Taking hold of a branch of a tree that leaned over the garden wall, the master gave it a good shake, sending autumn leaves cascading every which way onto the pristinely raked sand. "There," said the old master, "Now, it's perfect."

I don't know the origin of this story, which I first read in Janwillem Van de Wetering's *An Empty Mirror* when I was just beginning to practice. Looking back now, I am surprised to see that the primary lesson the author draws is one of impermanence and detachment. We should be prepared to see all our efforts come to nothing, and view the results with equanimity. Now, after years of sitting, that looks to me like a very unreal goal. I'd hate to think that practice is simply a matter of cultivating imperturbability or indifference. Today, I'd approach the story from a slightly different angle.

I think all of us who come to practice resemble that monk in one way or another. We want practice to settle our minds and allow us to rake and manicure our inner mental landscape into something serene and beautiful. We want to gather up and discard all the leaves of our unwanted thoughts and emotions. We want to attain a certain state or look and stay there. Imperturbability itself looks to me like just another version of that perfectly raked garden. Sooner or later, life is going to teach us that we can't hold on to any one state of mind. Here, the old master seems a little sadistic, shaking the tree just to unsettle the young monk. Or at least that's how it would feel from the monk's point of view, because he can't yet believe the garden really does look better with all those leaves scattered randomly about.

Now we might say that if the garden actually does look better unraked, why go to all the trouble of raking it in the first place? But the fact is, we are psychologically unprepared to simply accept life as it is. Unless we first meticulously rake the garden, we can't have the experience of seeing the perfection of the leaves falling where they may. What is the practice equivalent of this raking? Well, first of all, a careful awareness and labeling of our thoughts about just how we want our inner landscape to look. Just what we're willing to tolerate or not tolerate and where.

When I told this story to my wife, she laughed and said, "Sam is your old master! He can really shake your tree!" And she's right! Before our son Sam arrived on the scene, we lived in a neat, orderly apartment. Now the apartment is in a state of managed chaos—toys get scattered about, juice gets spilled, something is always in danger of being knocked over. These are the leaves that he scatters in my garden. There are days when all this seems perfectly normal—Sam is just doing what's natural for a two-year-old to do, and we are just doing what parents everywhere do, picking up after him and gradually trying to teach him what's OK to do and what isn't. Other days, we tear out our hair and I wonder aloud whether there are any boarding schools that accept toddlers. Last summer, we all took a trip to Italy. If you've ever traveled with a small child you can imagine what that was like. Generally, things went pretty smoothly whenever I could forget the word "vacation." Because "vacation" to me implies all the peace and quiet and time to read and write that a toddler completely disrupts. So Sam *is* a good teacher, always ready to point out to me whenever I become too attached to my perfectly raked garden and fail to see the perfection in the randomly scattered leaves.

We all have to practice raking that garden over and over, then watching the leaves fall and noticing how we react. Our practice isn't about clearing out the leaves once and for all; it's about building a bigger and bigger garden so it can hold more and more leaves, until it can contain whatever happens in our life. And when the garden expands to include our whole world—when we're truly willing to accept and respond to each moment of life as it is—then one day we find that every leaf has fallen in exactly the right place.

CHAPTER THIRTEEN

FORM AND NO FORM

THE ORDINARY MIND ZENDO is a center for lay practice.
I am not a monk or a priest. There are no robes or
shaved heads to make us look the part of Zen students. My teacher,
Joko Beck, used to say to anyone coming to her asking for ordination, "If you're serious about wanting to be a monk, just act like
one!" Although she herself received "Joko" as a Dharma name from
her Japanese teacher, Hakuyu Taizan Maezumi Roshi, she did not
continue the practice of giving her own students a new Zen name.
Traditionally, this is done as part of the Jukai ceremony. The Buddhist precepts originated as the rules that governed the life of the
sangha, the community of monks who gathered around the Buddha.
Today, in our group, rather than making them the basis for formal
monastic vows, we study them as a way of examining the role of
ethics, social engagement, and tradition in our daily lives. During
the Jukai ceremony as I perform it, the student receives his or her
own real name—not a Japanese one—as a "new" Dharma name,
symbolizing the identity of practice and ordinary life.

If you read about how Zen has traditionally been practiced over
the centuries in China and Japan, or have had the chance to practice at monastically oriented Zen centers, you know that traditional
Zen practice has been very rigorous indeed, usually centered around
week-long sesshins of great intensity. And if you compare that with
the weekly schedule at the Ordinary Mind Zendo, you might come

away with the idea that we're just practicing some brand of Zen Lite!

There used to be an analogous controversy within psycho-analysis. Isn't analysis "real" only if the patient lies on the couch or comes four or five times a week? Isn't once-a-week therapy inevitably a poor substitute for the "real thing"? Well, after many years of practicing therapy and analysis, I can say that I've seen many people whose lives were radically transformed during the course of a once-a-week therapy, and I have seen analysands lie on the couch four times week, year after year, and go nowhere at all. Obviously real practice doesn't come down to just logging as many hours as humanly possible facing a wall. In fact, I'd say real practice isn't about what happens in a zendo at all. It isn't about how many sesshins you sit, or even about what experiences you have on the cushion. Real practice is about how you face your life.

What we do in Zen practice, what we do in therapy, is watch how we go about facing—and even more important, *avoid* facing—our life as it is. And no experience in the zendo or insight in therapy is worth much if it doesn't address this basic issue. I remember twenty-five years ago, I somehow convinced my medical school to allow me to take off three months for elective training in what was then called the "human potential movement." Initially, I was very impressed by the intense feelings and early memories unleashed in the various Gestalt and Reichian weekend intensives I attended. But the next month, it seemed the same people would be back with the same basic problems and go through it all over again. There was an enormous, almost addictive appeal to the intensity unleashed in those workshops, but, all too often, apparently little translation of that insight into everyday behavior. And over the years I saw the same kind of thing happen at Zen retreats: intense experiences, but too often little change for the better in people's daily life. What I've come to believe is that the most effective form of practice for most people is a steady, day-in, day-out practice, month after month, year after year, one that doesn't emphasize the intensity or "special effects" that we all seem to crave. A regular, uneventful, unobtrusive daily sitting practice offers little reinforcement to our self-centered desire to be somebody special. We sit each morning the way we brush our teeth. This is nothing to boast about, nothing that anyone can't do.

While there are vibrant monastic traditions and authentic monastic vocations in contemporary America, I am no longer convinced that monastic Zen needs to be the sole benchmark of authentic practice. Most of the people who can benefit from practice will never become monks, and their practice should not be centered around finding time to leave their jobs or families for occasional intensive retreats. Certainly, we should never feel that "real" practice is something that is available only to a privileged few, or is possible only under special conditions. Practice is about how we live our lives, not about how to escape them in order to have a spiritual interlude in some exotic monastic setting. Integrating a sitting practice with a long-term psychoanalytic psychotherapy has proven to be one way to ensure that practice remains grounded in our daily lives. Sesshins can be powerful tools, but only when practice is firmly grounded in everyday life are the insights that arrive likely to be unobtrusively integrated into how life is actually lived. Uchiyama Roshi has written:

> To fall in love is ecstasy, but marriage is everyday life. Everyday life has rainy days, windy days, and stormy days. So you can't always be happy. It's the same with zazen. There are two kinds of zazen transmitted in Japan. One understands zazen as ecstasy and the other understands zazen as everyday life.
>
> A basic concept in Buddhism is that subject and object are one. The significance of this depends on whether you interpret the samadhi of oneness as a psychological condition of ecstasy that mystically

transcends the limits of "everyday mind" or whether
you actually practice it in your daily life.

A style of practice that is too centered on special experiences often
breeds an ego-attachment to the meditator's own specialness: to pride
in accomplishment, mastery, endurance, or spirituality. For someone
addicted to specialness, our ordinary day-in, day-out practice seems
too ordinary. But in fact it is *too difficult* for such individuals to tolerate that ordinariness, as it provides none of the ego-goodies that
they've come to expect from the mastery of difficulty and the achieve-
ment of intense "ecstatic" moments. (Not that these don't occur. They
are the almost inevitable by-product of steady sitting.) But a certain
type of student comes here, takes one look around, and quickly wants
to move on to the most rigorous, most intense, most "real" Zen they
can find! But a practice that doesn't gratify the sense of our own specialness may be the hardest—and most real—of all.

Zen is, on the one hand, simply the act of sitting and paying attention. On the other, it is a foreign tradition with more than two thousand
years of history behind it. A teaching that has been transmitted outside
of words and scriptures, it has nonetheless accumulated an enigmatic
and esoteric literature around itself, along with elaborate rituals built up
over centuries of practice in a variety of Asian monastic settings. American Zen can take the form either of a transplanted Japanese monastery
or a suburban house indistinguishable from its Southern Californian
neighbors. My own Ordinary Mind Zendo currently occupies an office
in a Greenwich Village apartment building. In one office, I meet with
patients; the adjacent office has been turned into a zendo.

Although the form of traditional Zen practice—no less than the
use of the couch in a traditional psychoanalysis—may strike some
as arbitrary, authoritarian, or artificial, it is only through the skillful
use of forms, discipline, and relationship that liberating change can
occur. This is just as true for psychoanalysis as it is for Zen. We

need the form of the zendo or of the analytic hour to get our attention and to hold it. The free, non–self-centered use of form is the true formlessness, or *no-form*. In Zen, we often hear the phrases *just doing* and *not doing* used interchangeably to indicate functioning free from separation or self-centeredness. Just sit. Speak without using your lips. "Not knowing" needn't imply dumbstruck wonder; it can also be the non–self-centered, spontaneous, and *expert* response to whatever arises, whether it takes the form of a swordsman skillfully parrying a blow or a doctor making a correct diagnosis.

Wittgenstein claimed that philosophy left everything just as it found it. Philosophy doesn't create a new, more precise language to replace the one we already speak. Rather, it helps us pay attention to what is already right in front of us and teaches us to examine how our language actually works. Zen, too, leaves everything alone. But for most of us, leaving things alone turns out to be hard work! Without the hard work, we don't seem able to leave our life alone and *just live*. Faced with the dilemma of suffering, consciously and unconsciously, we seek an antidote or an escape. And by seeking to escape our suffering we turn our life inside out, contorting our "ordinary mind" into an "isolated mind" that seeks to distance, control, and dissociate an inner "me" from outer pain. We chase after enlightenment or other special states of consciousness that will relieve all suffering and guarantee perfect happiness, or so we've heard. Whether our project is the flight from pain or the pursuit of happiness, the outcome is the same: a life in flight from itself and from this moment. And this moment turns out to be the only answer there is, the only self there is, the only teacher, and the only reality. All hidden in plain sight.

Zen practice, especially when united with the dynamic insights of psychoanalysis, offers us this paradox: a discipline that promises freedom, a hierarchical relationship that fosters true independence, a form that gives formlessness, a transformation that allows everything to be just as it is.

"ORDINARY MIND IS THE TAO"

The Case

Chao-chou asked Nan-ch'üan, "What is the Tao?"

Nan-ch'üan said, "Ordinary mind is the Tao."

Chao-chou asked, "Should I try to direct myself toward it?"

Nan-ch'üan said, "If you try to direct yourself you betray your own practice."

Chao-chou asked, "How can I know the Tao if I don't direct myself?"

Nan-ch'üan said, "The Tao is not subject to knowing or not knowing. Knowing is delusion; not knowing is blankness. If you truly reach the genuine Tao, you will find it as vast and boundless as outer space. How can this be discussed at the level of affirmation and negation?"

With these words, Chao-chou had sudden realization.

Wu-men's Comment

Questioned by Chao-chou, Nan-ch'üan lost no time in showing the smashed tile and the melted ice, where no explanation is possible. Though Chao-chou had realization, he could confirm it only after another thirty years of practice.

> *Spring comes with flowers, autumn with the moon,*
> *summer with breeze, winter with snow.*
> *When idle concerns don't hang in your mind,*
> *that is your best season.*

We have studied the words of wise old Chao-chou in the koans on Mu and "Wash Your Bowl." We have seen him in the midst of his training in the case "Nan-ch'üan Kills the Cat." Now we will bid him farewell by coming around full circle to this story from the very beginning days of his Zen practice. Here he is as a young monk, asking Nan-ch'üan for instruction. "What is the Tao?" Chao-chou asks, using a lofty word to connote the Great Way he's seeking. How do you tell someone that the Great Way is the sidewalk right under their feet? Nan-ch'üan tries, "Ordinary mind is the Tao." If you think of the Tao as something lofty and spiritual, what could be further from it than your ordinary mind? Our practice is all about our struggle to reconcile this seeming paradox. If this is it, why doesn't it *feel* like it? What were you expecting?

"Should I try to direct myself toward it?" If ordinary mind is the Way, how do I practice? Chao-chou wants to know. Nan-ch'üan replies, "If you try to direct yourself you betray your own practice." To go after something assumes that you don't already have it. What chance then do you have of finding it? But the problem of effort is a real one. We do make an effort in practice, but not the kind of effort we are used to thinking of, like the effort of going on a diet, when we try to become something we're not. Our effort is simply one of attention and honesty in seeing who and what we already are. And what we see is that we're constantly expending great effort every day trying to *escape* who and what we are to become something else, something special. But, as Sawaki Roshi said, "To make an ordinary person great is not the goal of Buddha's teaching."

What are your associations to the word *ordinary*? For many people that I see, *ordinary* is a pejorative—they want to be anything but ordinary. Too often, it seems, we feel misunderstood, not paid attention to, or underappreciated. We imagine that the only way to get the attention we crave is to stand out in some way, to become famous or extraordinary. Where I live in Manhattan, many middle-class families send their children to private preschools where the competition for admission can be quite fierce. Parents of two-year-olds fill out elaborate application forms and they and the child must be interviewed to gain a place in the most prestigious of these nursery schools, which are viewed as the first step on the ladder to the "right" kindergarten and elementary school. My wife showed me one of these applications, in which we were asked to fill out a page indicating "what was special" about our child. I suggested we write that our son was just an ordinary kid. They probably never had one of those apply before! (She wouldn't let me, of course, and has kept such applications away from me ever since.)

Our response to being called ordinary is one sign of how at peace we are with who we are. The Dalai Lama, regarded as an incarnation of the Bodhisattva of Compassion by the Tibetan people, describes himself as just an ordinary monk. Through both psychoanalysis and Zen practice we strive to come back to ourselves, to re-own what has been split off, and to embrace what we have warded off. Then we are who we are; each moment is what it is. We no longer have to pass our lives through the sieve of approval or disapproval, of "affirmation and negation." Life as it is stretches out before us, "as vast and boundless as outer space." Many commentators on this koan warn us, as does Aitken Roshi, that Nan-ch'üan's "ordinary mind" is "not the commonplace mind of self-centered preoccupation." If it were, there would be no need to practice. To leave everything just as it is, is a radical step for human beings, who sometimes seem incapable of leaving anything as they've found it. To eat when we're hungry and sleep when we're tired describes a simplicity that often eludes us without years of rigorous practice. It is indeed, as the Shakers used to sing, "a gift to be simple." It is the underlying simplicity of Bankei's Unborn: an ordinary mind that spontaneously recognizes the difference between crows and sparrows—always present, but obscured by our preoccupation with knowing and not knowing.

But we must be careful not to set up ordinariness, or simplicity, or "acting naturally" as some new special state of mind that we are striving to achieve. That, indeed, would be to "betray your own practice." Everywhere we turn, the gateless barrier is wide open. The Way continues under our feet even as we're lost in our self-centered dream, but only when we wake up do we see that it has been there all along. The mind you have at this very moment is your gate. If you are willing to enter through pain and confusion, it will never be locked.

When we stop trying to run away from our own mind, the *content* of our mind is no longer the problem. In the initial session of psychoanalysis, the new patient is traditionally told simply to say whatever comes to mind, without censoring or holding anything back. When the patient is finally able to follow that simple rule—usually after many years of working through a lifetime of inhibition and expectation—the analysis is over. What has changed? Everything and nothing.

Our usual lifelong struggle to bury or transcend, if not murder, those aspects of our own minds we find frightening or shameful leaves us exhausted, ragged from a constant internal struggle. Yet we stay continually worried and preoccupied lest some unacceptable or vulnerable part of ourselves remains undefended. Strangely enough, the aspects of ourselves of which we are most frightened are the very things we have most in common. They are the most ordinary things in the world: our hopes and fears, our yearnings for love and attention, our shame at our all-too-human failings, our simple mortality and fallibility. The Way beneath our feet is the path of life as it is. That life includes suffering, and suffering drives each one of us to look for a way out. But there is no way out—only a way in. When we realize there is no way out of life, we simultaneously realize all of life is our Way. But actualizing that realization, learning to truly inhabit our own skins, to be fully present in our own lives moment after moment is the work of a lifetime.

No wonder Wu-men says that Chao-chou needed another thirty

years of practice to confirm what he realized in his dialogue with Nan-ch'üan. Our day-in, day-out practice, no matter how deep our realization, is to stay aware of our tendency to subtly betray that realization by picking and choosing how each moment should go. It takes a long time to be willing to inhabit each and every moment, no matter what it brings—flowers in spring, the moon in autumn, or snow in winter. Perhaps only someone that we call a Buddha is completely at home in the world moment after moment. My teacher always insisted that she was no Buddha and that her own practice was far from over. Yet to fully accept one's humanity, one's limitations, and one's need for a lifetime of practice is perhaps another of Buddha's hallmarks.

In my own life, as a result of my practice of psychoanalysis and Zen, the roles that anger and fear play in my life have greatly diminished. But they cannot be banished once and for all. They promptly appear in a dozen barely noticeable ways every day, in all the little predilections and irritations that pop up in daily urban life. Minds are like that. Minds are also as vast and boundless as the empty sky. There is no limit to the number of clouds that sky can contain. A mind that no longer seeks to transcend itself, or hopes to banish the clouds from the sky—a mind that can allow itself to be ordinary—is special indeed. No longer preoccupied with our own condition, we respond freely to each moment, and there is no boundary to what we are.

Then, in the words of Torei Zenji's Bodhisattva's Vow:

> On each moment's flash of our thought
> there will grow a lotus flower
> and on each lotus flower will be revealed perfection
> unceasingly manifest as our life,
> just as it is,
> right here and right now.

NOTES

p. 2 [A collection of essays...grew out of a conference in Cuernavaca in 1957.] Fromm, Suzuki, and de Martino, *Zen Buddhism and Psychoanalysis*.

p. 3 [The impetus behind the conference...Karen Horney.] Horney had engaged in dialogues with D.T. Suzuki earlier in the decade, but died before the Cuernavaca conference.

p. 3 ["If we stay within the Freudian system....underlies humanistic psychoanalysis."] E. Fromm, "Psychoanalysis and Zen Buddhism," in Fromm, Suzuki, and de Martino, *Zen Buddhism and Psychoanalysis*, 86.

p. 5 [These new schools...offering a relational model.] See Mitchell, *Relational Concepts in Psychoanalysis*.

p. 5 ["like one foot forward and the other behind in walking."] Suzuki, *Branching Streams Flow in the Darkness*, 191. *Sandokai* is a poem composed by Sekito Kisen (Jap. for Shitou Xiqian, 700–790), sometimes translated as "The Identity of Relative and Absolute," and chanted during services in Soto Zen temples.

p. 7 [The parable of the mother tiger and her cubs.] For the origin of this parable see Aitken, *Gateless Barrier*, Case 15: Tung-shan's Sixty Blows.

p. 9 [Jeffrey Rubin and Michael Eigen have documented...meditation itself served to reinforce defensive patterns.] Rubin, *Psychotherapy and Buddhism;* Eigen, *Psychoanalytic Mystic*.

p. 13 [Karen Horney led a cohort...singing, "Let My People Go!"] Schwartz, *Cassandra's Daughters*, 188.

p. 13 [He thought of himself as Mr. Psychoanalysis.] Kohut, "On Empathy," 526.

p. 14 [Freud "gazed at man's inner life...the theoretical framework of psychoanalysis."] Kohut, *Restoration of the Self*, 67.

p. 15 ["Men's knowledge of the external world....must therefore be in error."] Berlin, *Vico and Herder*, xvii.

p. 15 [Empathy itself, Kohut claimed, "is a therapeutic action...in the broadest sense of the word."] Kohut, "On Empathy," 530.

p. 22 ["The intersubjective context has a constitutive role in *all* forms of psychopathology."] Stolorow and Atwood, *Contexts of Being*, 3.

p. 31 The case and Wu-men's comment and verse are from Aitken, *Gateless Barrier*, 7–9.

p. 37 [Dogen says, "Now sit steadfastly...the essential art of zazen."] Tanahashi, *Enlightenment Unfolds,* 33.

p. 38 [John Daido Loori Roshi...maintains he is simply following Dogen's own practice.] Loori, *Two Arrows Meeting in Mid-Air*, 19–20.

p. 38 [Foulk claims that in "medieval Japanese monasteries...in the manner of the 'Zen of contemplating phrases.'"] Foulk, "Form and Function of Koan Literature," 25.

p. 38 [scholars agree that Dogen would have rejected any "instrumentalist"...kensho.] Kim, *Dogen Kigen*; Hori, G.V.S. "Koan and Kensho in the Rinzai Zen Curriculum" in *The Koan,* ed. S. Heine and D. Wright. New York: Oxford University Press, 2000.

p. 40 [The goal of philosophy is to show the fly the way out of the fly-bottle.] Wittgenstein, *Philosophical Investigations*, PI 309, p. 103: "What is your aim in philosophy?—To shew the fly the way out of the fly-bottle."

p. 43 ["limitlessness and of a bond to the universe" as the "oceanic feeling."] Freud, *Civilization and Its Discontents*, 68. See Silverman, Lachmann, and Milich, *The Search for Oneness*, for an overview of this literature.

p. 43 [William James...treated religious experience as important...self.] James, *The Varieties of Religious Experience.*

p. 44 ["Through meditation....to the somato-symbiotic phase of the mother-child relationship."] Shafii, "Silence in the Service of the Ego," 442.

p. 45 ["self and other...make up an interpenetrating field."] Eigen, "Area of Faith." In this article Eigen offers his version of D. W. Winnicott's notion of a transitional space as part of infant development.

p. 52 The case and Wu-men's comment and verse are from Aitken, *Gateless Barrier*, 132.

p. 53 Wittgenstein, L., *Philosophical Investigations*, 243–57; pp. 88–92.

p. 53 ["One of the most useful and misleading words....there is no (real) exclamation."] Blyth, *Zen and the Classics*, 89–90.

p. 55 [the emptiness to which a fragile, poorly structured self is prone bears little relation to the Buddhist use of that word.] Jack Engler was one of the first to point out the confusion between these uses of the term *emptiness;* see his "Therapeutic Aims in Psychotherapy and Meditation."

p. 58 ["If this house were to burn down....I would really suffer."] Aitken, "Onto the Next Project!" 19.

p. 58 ["Impermanence is, in fact, just another name for perfection."] Beck, *Everday Zen*, 110.

p. 59 The case and Wu-men's comment and verse are from Aitken, *Gateless Barrier*, 60.

p. 60 ["Aristotle described the soul using the metaphor of a candle."] Aristotle, *De Anima* II.1.412b 5–9. "That is why we can dismiss as unnecessary the question whether the soul and the body are one: it is as though we were to ask whether the wax and its shape are one, or generally the matter of a thing and that of which it is the matter." (J. Barnes (ed.), *The Complete Works of Aristotle: The Revised Oxford Translation*.)

p. 64 ["If I am told 'Joko, you have one more day to live,'...is this OK with me?"] Beck, *Everyday Zen*, 115.

p. 64 ["that I don't scream, or cry....whatever they may be, that is it."] Ibid., 115–16.

p. 66 ["This very moment...your original face before the birth of your parents."] See Aitken's discussion of *Wu-men Kuan*, case 23, in *Gateless Barrier*, 152–54.

p. 67 ["would like the Zen koan…something originary shines through."] Eigen, *Psychoanalytic Mystic*, 34.

p. 68 ["The time has probably come….one jump ahead of reality."] Merton, *Dancing in the Water of Life*, 95.

p. 69 ["break(s) down the distinction between intrinsic and extrinsic….just one more nexus of relations."] Rorty, "A World without Substances or Essences," 50, 53–54.

p. 69 ["rejects the commonsense impression…of an autonomous nature."] Cook, *Hua-yen Buddhism*, 41.

p. 70 ["But once we are able to perceive….any other kind of person."] Ibid.

p. 71 ["emotions are not simply blind surges….ways of interpreting the world."] Nussbaum, *Therapy of Desire*, 369.

p. 72 ["The feelings that go with the experience of emotion….helpful and noxious."] Ibid., 369–70.

p. 73 ["Drop a coin in the river, and look for it in the river."] Tanahashi, *Enlightenment Unfolds*, 103. This phrase is also found among the sayings of Yunmen (864–949), who lived three hundred years before Dogen, but I do not know whether he originated it or if it was proverbial then as well.

p. 78 [three main areas of this alienation: from nature, social life, subjectivity.] Atwood and Stolorow, "Defects in the Self," 8, 9, 11.

p. 78 [Zen directly confronts…aspects of the myth of the isolated mind.] See Magid, "Surface, Depth and the Isolated Mind."

p. 78 ["At the time when an individual's self…a lifeplan for the self."] Wolf, E. *Treating the Self*, 51. For the notion of a false self, see Winnicott, *Maturational Processes*.

Wolf explains "the whole configuration of poles and tension arc" in this way: "Kohut conceptualized the emerging self as having a *bipolar* structure. By that he meant that during the structural organization of these experiences they became clustered into two structural locations, according to their mirroring or idealizing character. Thus the emerging self could be thought to have two poles.... The basic ambitions for power and success emanate from [one]. The other pole precipitates out of idealizing experiences and harbors the basic idealized goals. An intermediate area of basic talents and skills are activated by the *tension arc* that establishes itself between ambitions and skill" (31).

p. 79 ["True self is nothing at all....An absence of what?"] Beck, *Everyday Zen*, 101.

p. 79 [a "no-person psychology."] Stolorow, "Principles of Dynamic Systems," 867.

p. 79 ["To carry the self forward...the self is awakening."] Tanahashi, *Enlightenment Unfolds*, 35.

p. 81 ["quest for self-development...felt flawed and inadequate"; "role of...healing wounded sparrows."] Rubin, *Psychotherapy and Buddhism*, 98.

p. 81 ["focused on detaching....thus unfortunately stifled."] Ibid., 107.

p. 83 ["Do not think you'll recognize your own enlightenment."] I employ the locution "an old teacher said..." whenever I am unable to remember whom I'm quoting.

p. 83 ["gain is...enlightenment."] Uchiyama, K., *Refining Your Life*, 96.

p. 84 The case and Wu-men's comment and verse are from Aitken, *Gateless Barrier*, 81.

p. 88 [a succession of isolated minds, each in a different "relational configuration."] Mitchell, "Contemporary Perspectives on Self," 128.

p. 89 ["While all of you here are turned toward me...the Buddha Mind that is unborn."] Haskel, *Bankei Zen*, 75.

p. 90 ["All delusions...whether it is or not."] Ibid., 24.

p. 90 ["pre-reflective unconscious" and the "dynamic unconscious."] Stolorow and Atwood, *Contexts of Being*, 33.

p. 91 [The surest way to be trapped...perceive reality "directly."] Bateson and Bateson, *Angels Fear*, 54.

p. 92 ["rigidified structures that impede fluid engagement with one's surround"; "such as between lovers...overrides each one's fear."] Ringstrom,

P. "Discussion of Magid's 'Your Ordinary Mind' in Safran, J. (ed.), *Psychoanalysis and Buddhism* (Boston: Wisdom Publications, forthcoming).

p. 93 [Huang-po…is even said to have slapped the emperor.] Cleary, *Secrets of the Blue Cliff Record*, 40.

p. 93 [Austin concludes that his experience "reveals innate neurophysiological capacities."] Austin, *Zen and the Brain*, 600.

p. 94 [Bion "calls on us to face the fact…whatever level of processing we tap."] Eigen, *Psychoanalytic Mystic*, 99–100.

p. 94 ["Plenty of people will tell you….Don't you believe it."] Whalen, *Imaginary Speeches*, 19.

p. 95 ["The self is still present…washes the dishes and puts them away."] Aitken, *Original Dwelling Place*, 49.

p. 96 The case and Wu-men's comment and verse are from Aitken, *Gateless Barrier*, 94.

p. 101 [In Kohut's self psychology…*compensatory structure* is established.] Kohut, "Restoration of the Self."

p. 101 [restructuring the ego ideal as "transvaluation."…dissolving of old structures.] Meissner, *Ignatius of Loyola*, 398, 395.

p. 102 […Kohut's own notion of "optimal frustration."] Kohut, "Analysis of the Self."

p. 102 [a more nurturing stance of "optimal responsiveness."] Bacal, "Optimal Responsiveness."

p. 104 ["building a bigger container."] Beck, *Everyday Zen*, 50.

p. 105 ["affect-integrating, containing and modulating intersubjective context."] Stolorow and Atwood, *Contexts of Being*, 54.

p. 106 [Psychoanalysis cures by "providing missing developmental experiences…the repetitive dimension of the transference."] Atwood and Stolorow, "Defects in the Self," 521–22.

p. 107 ["Lost in raking the leaves…his original face was apparent to him."] See Aitken, *Gateless Barrier*, 39.

p. 108 [Three times Linji asked…and three times his teacher hit him.] See Cleary, *Book of Serenity*, case 86.

p. 110 ["all the myriad things come forth."] Tanahashi, *Enlightenment Unfolds*, 35.

p. 116 ["No!…Zazen is useless."] Uchiyama, *Zen Teaching*, 123.p. 118 [Japanese masters who vigorously supported…wholeheartedly into battle.] Victoria, *Zen at War*.

p. 119 ["Its head, horns, and four legs…tail pass through as well?"] Aitken, *Gateless Barrier*, 231.

p. 124 ["In the middle of a solemn service…it doesn't matter, does it?"] Uchiyama, *Zen Teaching*, 53–54.

p. 125 The case and Wu-men's comment and verse are from Aitken, *Gateless Barrier*, 54.

p. 131 [they compassionately offered their students…already peeled and ready to swallow] Aitken, *Gateless Barrier*, 1991.

p. 131 [Luzu…responded…by turning his back to them and silently facing the wall.] Cleary, *Book of Serenity*, Case 23, 100–103.

p. 132 ["he'd read some books about Zen….sensed authority and humility."] Chadwick, *Crooked Cucumber*, 171–72.

p. 132 ["The last words of the Buddha…this authority, is everywhere."] Beck, *Everyday Zen*, 15–16.

p. 133 Deborah Norden (1954–94), architect and illustrator of Guy Davenport's *Belinda's World Tour*, which we hand printed together. After her death, I married Sharon Dolin, a poet and the mother of our son, Sam.

p. 134 ["Zen practice…act of uniting with something."] Quoted in Aitken, *Original Dwelling Place*, 81.

p. 134 [Echoing…your ordinary mind is the way."] See Aitken, *Gateless Barrier*, Case 19, 126.

p. 136 [recursive functions…to fractal geometries.] Mandelbrot, *Fractal Geometry of Nature*.

p. 141 Wind Bell 7, no. 28, 1968; quoted in Beck, *Everyday Zen*, 110.

p. 146 [Some colleagues have also raised…professional boundaries.] Joseph Bobrow, personal communication.

p. 148 ["Embracing the concept…availability to the child."] Orange, *Emotional Understanding*, 127.

p. 149 [There is by now…and group therapy.] For an overview from a self psychological and intersubjective vantage point, see Harwood and Pines (eds.), "Self Experiences in Group: Intersubjective and Self Psychological Pathways to Human Understanding."

p. 150 ["While I was well aware…and not as patients."] Downing, *Shoes Outside the Door,* p. 229.

p. 151 [Freud…went so far as to analyze his own daughter.] Roazen, *How Freud Worked.*

p. 152 ["As Dharma heir…in every detail of my life."] Steve Wintraub in Downing, *Shoes Outside the Door,* p. 237.

p. 152 ["The roshi had reached the point…what he's doing."] Yvonne Rand to Gary Snyder. Downing, *Shoes Outside the Door,* p. 253.

p. 161–62 ["To fall in love is ecstasy…practice it in your daily life."] Uchiyama, *Zen Teaching,* 52.

p. 163 Wittgenstein, L., *Philosophical Investigations,* PI 124: "Philosophy may in no way interfere with the actual use of language; it can in the end only describe it…. It leaves everything as it is."

p. 164 The case and Wu-men's comment and verse are from Aitken, *Gateless Barrier,* 126–27.

p. 166 ["not the commonplace mind of self-centered preoccupation."] Aitken, *Gateless Barrier,* 128.

p. 168 [Torei Zenji's (1721–92) Bodhisattva's Vow] from Aitken, *Original Dwelling Place,* 176–77.

GLOSSARY

BUDDHIST TERMS

daisan. A formal interview with the teacher in which students can ask questions and present their state of mind to the teacher.

dharma. A momentary phenomenon. When capitalized, Dharma refers to the Buddha's teaching, based on his realization of the transitory, impermanent nature of all things (dharmas).

enlightenment. (1) A state of perfect, selfless, joyful, compassionate functioning; Buddhahood. (2) Life lived just as it is.

Jukai. An initiation ceremony for receiving the precepts.

kensho (Jap., "seeing true nature"). A moment of sudden realization; see *enlightenment.*

koan (Jap., "public case"). Typically a story of an interaction between a master and student in which the Dharma is made manifest. Over 1,700 classic koans are extant. These cases were later formally compiled and studied as part of Zen training. The two most famous koan collections are *The Gateless Barrier* (*Wu-men Kuan*) compiled by Wu-men (1183–1260) and *The Blue Cliff Record,* originally compiled by Hsüeh-tou (982–1052), with added commentary by Yuan-wu (1063–1135).

oryoki. A wrapped set of eating bowls and utensils used for formal meals during sesshin; also the formal meal itself.

samadhi. A meditative state of concentration or absorption.

sangha. The community of Buddhist practitioners.

sesshin (Jap., "to gather, touch, or convey the mind"). An extended period of intensive zazen practice.

teisho. A public talk by a Zen teacher.

zendo. Zen meditation hall.

PSYCHOANALYTIC TERMS

empathy. A mode of psychological inquiry based on imaginatively projecting oneself into the subjective experience of another. It emphasizes the importance of the patient's feeling understood as opposed to the analyst's acquisition of objective knowledge.

intersubjectivity theory. A branch of psychoanalysis, developed by Robert Stolorow and George Atwood, that emphasizes inquiry into the mutual influence, co-construction, and organization of both the analyst's and the patient's subjective experience within the therapeutic relationship.

relational theory. A branch of psychoanalysis, principally associated with the work of Stephen Mitchell (1946–2000), that developed as a synthesis of the interpersonal theories of American analyst Harry Stack Sullivan (1892–1949), and the British object relations school associated with W. Fairbairn (1889–1964), D.W. Winnicott (1896–1971), and W.R. Bion (1897–1979). It pictures the self as multiple and discontinuous, the sum of differing and often contradictory representations of oneself and others.

self psychology. A branch of psychoanalysis developed by Heinz Kohut (1913–81) that emphasizes the individual's fundamental developmental need to organize and regulate experience within a stable, meaningful, and cohesive configuration, the self. It also stresses the contextualized nature of all self experiences, and the lifelong need for affirming and vitalizing relationships and experiences (selfobjects).

selfobject. An individual or activity that is experienced as vitalizing, affirming, or stabilizing of one's self. Selfobject experiences may be *archaic* (highly specific and easily disrupted) or *mature* (nonspecific, easily generalizable, and stable).

transference. The reinstatement in the present of old patterns of relating and organizing experience. Two dimensions of transference should be distinguished: the *repetitive*, in which the dread of re-injury and the defenses used to ward it off are in the foreground; and the *selfobject*, in which longed-for developmental opportunities for empathic responsiveness and connection are reestablished.

REFERENCES

Aitken, R. *The Gateless Barrier*. San Francisco: North Point, 1991.

———. *Original Dwelling Place*. Washington, D.C.: Counterpoint, 1996.

———. "Onto the Next Project! An Interview with Mushim Ikeda-Nash." *Turning Wheel*, winter 2001, 18–21.

American Psychiatric Association. *Diagnostic Criteria from DSM-IV*. Washington, D.C., 1994.

Atwood, G., and R. Stolorow. "Defects in the Self: Liberating Concept or Imprisoning Metaphor?" *Psychoanalytic Dialogues* 7, no. 4 (1997): 517–22.

Austin, J. *Zen and the Brain*. Cambridge: MIT Press, 1998.

Bacal, H. "Optimal Responsiveness and the Therapeutic Process." In *Progress in Self Psychology,* vol. 1, ed. A. Goldberg, 202–27. Hillsdale, N.J.: Analytic Press, 1985.

Barnes, J. (ed.). *The Complete Works of Aristotle: The Revised Oxford Translation*. Princeton, NJ: Princeton University Press, 1984.

Bateson, G., and M. C. Bateson. *Angels Fear*. New York: Macmillan, 1987.

Beck, C. J. *Everyday Zen*. San Francisco: Harper, 1989.

Berlin, I. *Vico and Herder*. London: Hogarth Press, 1976.

Blyth, R H. *Zen and the Classics,* vol. 5, *Twenty-four Essays*. Tokyo: Hokuseido Press, 1962.

Brandchaft, B., and R. Stolorow. "The Borderline Concept:Pathological Character or Iatrogenic Myth?" In *Empathy II*, ed. J. Lichtenberg, M. Bornstein, and D. Silver. Hillsdale, NJ: Analytic Press, 1984, 337–57.

Chadwick, D. *Crooked Cucumber: The Life and Teaching of Shunryu Suzuki.* New York: Broadway Books, 1999.

Cleary, T. *The Book of Serenity.* Hudson, New York: Lindisfarne, 1990.

———. *Secrets of the Blue Cliff Record.* Boston: Shambhala, 2000.

Cook, F. *Hua-yen Buddhism.* University Park: Pennsylvania State University Press, 1977.

Dogen. *Shobogenzo.* Trans. K. Nishiyama. Tokyo: Nakayama Shobo, 1983.

Downing, M. *Shoes Outside the Door: Desire, Devotion and Excess at San Francisco Zen Center.* Washington, D.C.: Counterpoint. 2001.

Eigen, M. "Area of Faith in Winnicott, Lacan, and Bion." *International Journal of Psycho-Analysis* 62 (1981): 413–33.

———. *The Psychoanalytic Mystic.* London and New York: Free Association Books, 1998.

Engler, J. "Therapeutic Aims in Psychotherapy and Meditation: Developmental Stages in the Representation of the Self." *Journal of Transpersonal Psychology* 16 (1984): 25–61.

Foulk, T.G. "The Form and Function of Koan Literature: A Historical Overview." In *The Koan,* ed. S. Heine and D. Wright. New York: Oxford University Press, 2000, 15–45.

Freud, S. *Civilization and Its Discontents* (1930). In J. Strachey (ed. and trans.). *The Standard Edition of the Complete Psychological Works of Sigmund Freud,* vol. 21. London: Hogarth Press, 1953–74, 59–145.

Fromm, E., D.T. Suzuki, and R. de Martino. *Zen Buddhism and Psychoanalysis.* London: George Allen and Unwin, 1960.

Harwood, I., and M. Pines (eds.). *Self Experiences in Group: Intersubjective and Self Psychological Paths to Human Understanding.* London: J. Kingsley, 1998.

Haskel, P. *Bankei Zen.* New York: Grove, 1984.

Hori, G.V.S. "Koan and Kensho in the Rinzai Zen Curriculum." In *The Koan,* ed. S. Heine and D. Wright. New York: Oxford University Press, 2000, 280–315.

James, W. *The Varieties of Religious Experience.* New York: Longmans and Green, 1902.

Kim, Hee-Jin. *Dogen Kigen—Mystical Realist*. Tucson: University of Arizona Press, 1975.

Kohut, H. *The Analysis of the Self*. New York: International Universities Press, 1971.

———. *The Restoration of the Self*. New York: International Universities Press, 1977.

———. "On Empathy." (1981). In *Search for the Self*, ed. P. Ornstein. Madison, Conn.: International Universities, 525–35.

———. "Introspection, Empathy, and Psychoanalysis." In *The Search for the Self*, ed. P. Ornstein. Madison, CT: International Universities, 1991, 205–32.

Kornfield, J. *After the Ecstasy, the Laundry*. New York: Bantam Books, 2000.

Loori, J.D. *Two Arrows Meeting in Mid-Air*. Boston: Charles E. Tuttle, 1994.

Magid, B. "Surface, Depth and the Isolated Mind." In *Progress in Self Psychology*, vol. 15, ed. A. Goldberg. Hillsdale, NJ: Analytic Press, 1999.

Mandelbrot, B. *The Fractal Geometry of Nature*. NY: W. H. Freeman, 1977.

Meissner, W.W. *Ignatius of Loyola*. New Haven: Yale University Press, 1992.

Merton, T. *Dancing in the Water of Life*. New York: HarperCollins, 1997.

Mitchell, S. *Relational Concepts in Psychoanalysis*. Cambridge: Harvard University Press, 1983.

———. "Contemporary Perspectives on Self: Toward an Integration." *Psychoanalytic Dialogues* 1 (1991): 121–47.

Nussbaum, M. *The Therapy of Desire*. Princeton, NJ: Princeton University Press, 1994.

Orange, D. *Emotional Understanding*. New York: Guilford, 1995.

Ringstrom, P. "Discussion of Magid's 'Your Ordinary Mind.'" In *Psychoanalysis and Buddhism,* ed. J. Safran. Boston: Wisdom Publications, forthcoming.

Roazen, P. *How Freud Worked: First-Hand Accounts of Patients*. Northvale, NJ: Jason Aronson, 1995.

Rorty, R. "A World without Substances or Essences." In *Philosophy and Social Hope*. London: Penguin, 1999.

Rubin, J. *Psychotherapy and Buddhism: Toward an Integration.* New York: Plenum, 1996.

Safran, J., ed. *Psychoanalysis and Buddhism.* Boston: Wisdom Publications, forthcoming.

Schwartz, J. *Cassandra's Daughters.* New York: Viking, 1999.

Shafii, M. "Silence in the Service of the Ego: Psychoanalytic Study of Meditation." *International Journal of Psycho-Analysis* 54 (1973): 431–43.

Silverman, S., F. Lachmann, and R. Milich. *The Search for Oneness.* New York: International Universities, 1982.

Stolorow, R. "Principles of Dynamic Systems, Intersubjectivity, and the Obsolete Distinction between One-Person and Two-Person Psychologies." *Psychoanalytic Dialogues* 7 (1997): 859–68.

Stolorow, R., and G. Atwood. *Contexts of Being.* Hillsdale, NJ: Analytic Press, 1992.

Suzuki, S. *Branching Streams Flow in the Darkness.* Ed. M. Weitsman and M. Wenger. Berkeley and Los Angeles: University of California Press, 1999.

Tanahashi, Kazuaki. *Enlightenment Unfolds: The Essential Teachings of Zen Master Dogen.* Boston: Shambhala, 1999.

Uchiyama, K. *Refining Your Life.* Tokyo: Weatherhill, 1983.

———. *The Zen Teaching of "Homeless" Kodo Uchiyama.* N.p.: Libri on Demand, 2000.

Van de Wetering, J. *The Empty Mirror.* Boston: Houghton Mifflin, 1974.

———. *Afterzen.* New York: St. Martin's Press, 1999.

Victoria, B. *Zen at War.* New York: Weatherhill, 1997.

Whalen, P. *Imaginary Speeches for a Brazen Head.* Los Angeles: Black Sparrow, 1972.

Winnicott, D.W. *The Maturational Processes and the Facilitating Environment.* New York: International Universities Press, 1965.

Wittgenstein, L. *Philosophical Investigations.* London: Basil Blackwell, 1953.

Wolf, E. *Treating the Self.* New York: Guilford Press, 1988.

INDEX

A

acceptance
  of imperfection, 121, 123–24
  of impermanence, 57, 58
  of perfection, 124
  of self, 116–20, 165–66
affect regulation, 102–3
After the Ecstasy, the Laundry (Kornfield), 65
Afterzen (van de Wetering), 8
Aitken, Robert, 58, 95, 166
alienation, 77–78
anger in resistance, 35, 36, 127
Apology (Plato), 21
archaic selfobject experiences, 19
Aristotle, 60
attachment, 57, 72, 140–42
Atwood, George, 21, 77, 90
Austin, James, 56, 93
authority relationships, 129–33
awareness, ix–x, 5, 57

B

Baker, Richard, 146
Bankei, 88–90, 92–94, 117, 166
barriers, 31–33, 41–42, 162
Bateson, Gregory, 91
Beck, Joko
  the authority of the teacher, 132, 133
  on enlightenment, 63–64
  on impermanence, 58
  ordination practices, 159
  on practice, 104
  true self, 79

Zen practice of, 8
Berlin, Isiah, 14
Bion, W.R., 94, 134
blood pressure, 120–21
Blyth, R.H., 53
borderline personality disorder, 21, 136
bottom-up practice, 35–39
boundaries, 36–37, 83, 137–38, 146, 148, 150–51, 152
Brandchaft, Bernard, 21–22

C

change, 101–11
Chao-Chou's dog (koan), 26, 30–33
Chinese Shobogenzo (Dogen), 38
compassion, x, 60, 79–80
constancy and impermanence, 87–95
Cook, Francis, 69–70

D

daisan, defined, 175
Dalai Lama, 166
detachment, 140–42, 150
determinism, 120
developmental therapy model, 16–17
dharma, defined, 175
disappointment rewards, 122–23
Dogen
  "Encouraging Words", 73–75
  on repetition, 110
  on self, 79
  separation disappearance, 54
  Shobogenzo, 6
  think not-thinking, 37–38

on zazen, 116–17
Dorsey, Issan, 146
dualism
    described, 77
    in emotions, 106
    in mental health, 135–36
    oneness and, 45
    in psychoanalytic theory, 14, 22,
        45–47
    Zen practice and, 78
dynamic unconscious, 90

E
effort and acceptance related, 117
ego, 106, 117–18
Eigen, Michael, 8, 67, 134
Eightfold Path, 64–65
emotional essentialism, 70
emotional maturation, 20–21
emotions
    affect regulation of, 102–3
    anger as resistance, 35, 36, 127
    detachment in, 54
    dualism in, 106
    fear as resistance, 35, 36, 127
    nonessentialist approach to, 70–72
    the unconscious and, 91
empathic inquiry, 14
empathy, 14–15, 18, 20, 133–39, 176
emptiness (nonessentialism), 55–61.
    See also insight
An Empty Mirror (van de Wetering),
    150
"Encouraging Words" (Dogen), 73–75
enlightenment
    defined, 175
    life after, 65, 92–93, 123
    recognition of, 63–65, 82–83
essentialism/anti-essentialism, 68–72,
    87

F
family life, 161
fear in resistance, 35, 36, 127
Foulk, T. Griffith, 38

Freud, Sigmund, 13–14, 44, 147, 151
Freudian model
    analytic neutrality, 131
    the ego, 106
    of illness, 3
    Kohut and, 13–16, 22–23
    of the mind, 72
    of repetition, 109
    the unconscious, 90
Fromm, Erich, 3, 13
fulfillment, 79

G
The Gateless Barrier, 6, 30–31
The Gateless Gate, 31
genjokoan, 38
golf joke, 118–19
Goose in the Bottle (koan), 40–42

H
Horney, Karen, 13
Hsi-Chung builds carts (koan), 59–61
Hsiang-yen, 107
Huang-po, 93

I
idealizing selfobject transference, 19
impermanence
    in Buddha nature, 58
    in Buddhism, 123
    constancy and, 87–95
    detachment and, 141
    emptiness and, 56
    nonattachment and, 57
    as perfection, 58
insight, 26–27, 63–65, 67. See also
        emptiness; oneness
intersubjectivity theory, 22, 45, 176
"Introspection, Empathy and Psycho-
        analysis" (Kohut), 13
isolated mind, 77–83, 93, 163
It is not with the tongue that you
        speak (koan), 54

J

Jui-Yen calls "Master" (koan), 84–86
Jukai ceremony, 145, 159
just sitting (practice), 35–39

K
kensho (breakthrough)
  affect regulation in, 102–3
  defined, 175
  the koan and, 38
  perception in, 93
  perfection in, 124
  promise of, 7
  samadhi and, 56
koans
  about, 26
  challenges of, 101–2
  Chao-Chou's dog, 26, 30–33
  defined, 175
  enlightenment and, 38
  the Goose in the Bottle, 40–42
  history, 38
  Hsi-Chung builds carts, 59–61
  It is not with the tongue that you
    speak, 54
  Jui-Yen calls "Master", 84–86
  Mu, 25–26, 30–33
  Nan-Ch'üan Kills the Cat, 96–99
  Ordinary Mind is the Tao, 164–68
  Sung-Yüan's Person of Great
    Strength, 50–54
  Wash Your Bowl, 125–27
  What Shakes Your Tree?, 150–52
  What was your original face before
    you were born?, 66–67
  Why has the man of great satori not
    cut the red thread?, 54
  Wu-tsu's Buffalo Passes through the
    Window, 119
Kohut, Heinz, 13–21, 78, 101–2, 106
Kornfield, Jack, 65
Koun, Yamada, 134

L
language, contextual nature of, 40–41
Linji, 108

Loori, John Daido, 38
Luzu, 131

M
Maezumi, Hakuyu Taizan, 159
Mandelbrot patterns, 136
mature selfobject experiences, 19,
  20–21
meditation. See sitting (zazen)
Meissner, W.W., 101
Merton, Thomas, 68
mirroring selfobject transference, 19
Mitchell, Stephen, 87
Mu (koan), 25–26, 30–33

N
Nan-Ch'üan, 134
Nan-Ch'üan Kills the Cat (koan),
  96–99
narcissistic personality disorder,
  15–19, 136
no-self, 45–46, 63–72, 80–82. See also
  self-centeredness
no separation/nonseparation, 49–52,
  65. See also oneness; separation
non-self-centeredness, 80–82
nonessentialism (emptiness), 55–61
nuclear self, 78
Nussbaum, Martha, 71–72

O
Obaku, 93
Oedipal transference, 18
oneness (nondualism), 28, 37, 43–51,
  64. See also insight; separation/no
  separation
Orange, Donna, 148
ordinary mind, 163, 164–68
Ordinary Mind is the Tao (koan),
  164–68
Ordinary Mind Zendo, 159, 162
organizing principles of the unconscious. See the unconscious
oryoki, defined, 175

P
parenting, 19, 70–71, 112–13
peak experiences, 28–29, 49
perfection, 58, 67, 120, 123–24
Philosophical Investigations (Wittgen-
    stein), 40
post-enlightenment psychotherapy, 65
practice. *See* psychoanalysis; sitting
    (zazen)
pratityasamutpada, 69
pre-reflective unconscious, 90–92
Prozac, 121, 135–36
psychoanalysis. *See also* Zen psy-
    chotherapy similarities, differences
    emotional essentialism in, 70
    empathy in, 14–15, 18
    Freudian model, 13–16
    initial interview styles, 17–18
    introspection in, 14–15
    observation in, 14, 22
    post-enlightenment, 65
    sitting (zazen) integrated, 143–54
Psychoanalytic Mystic (Eigen), 134
psychoanalytic theory (dualistic),
    13–14, 22
psychotherapy practice, 2, 133–39,
    143–50

R
realization and attachment, 72
reason and emotion, 71
"Recommending Zazen to All People"
    (Dogen), 37
regression, 43–45, 46–47, 153
relational theory, defined, 176
relationships (student-teacher), 9–10,
    106, 129–33
repetition, role of, 108–11
resistance
    to acceptance, 58
    attachment and, 57
    bodily responses to, 104, 126–27
    emotion in, 35, 36, 127
    in "just sitting" practice, 35, 43
    nonseparation and, 50

in psychoanalysis, 58
repetition and, 110
responsibility, 60
The Restoration of the Self (Kohut), 17
Ringstrom, Phillip, 91–92
ritual and nonseparation, 50
Rorty, Richard, 68–69
Rubin, Jeffrey, 8, 81

S
samadhi, 56, 80, 110, 176
San Francisco Zen Center, 146, 152
sangha, defined, 176
Sawaki, Kodo, 83, 116, 118
Scienza Nuova (Vico), 14
self-acceptance, 116–20, 121,
    123–24, 165–66
self-centeredness. *See also* no-self
    absence of, 80–82
    as barrier, 41–42
    defined, 79
    dropping away of, x, 93
    repetition and, 109–10
    the Unborn and, 92–93
    the unconscious and, 89–93, 101–2,
        106–8, 119
    uselessness of zazen and, 118
self psychology, 20, 22–23, 45, 46,
    176
self/the self
    acceptance of, 116–20, 121,
        123–24, 165–66
    anti-essentialist perspective, 68–70,
        87
    boundaries of, 137–38
    in Buddhism, 106
    contextual nature of, 40–41, 45
    defined by Kohut, 21
    and emptiness, 55–61
    essential nature of, 66–69, 87–88
    intersubjectivity theory and, 22–23,
        45
    no-self and, 45–46, 63–72, 79,
        80–82
    nuclear self, 78

and oneness, 43–51
self-centeredness and, 79
separation and, 94
true self, 66–72, 79, 82–83
selfobject, 18–22, 46, 55, 106, 177
separation/no separation. *See also* one-
    ness
barriers in, 31–33
body perception in, 52–54
boundaries, 36
of dualism, 45–47, 50–51
of emotions, 54
in everyday life, 49–50
and Mu, 26
realization of, 65
ritual in, 50
self and the world, 94
sesshin, defined, 176
sexual relationships with
    students/patients, 147, 150, 151
Shakyamuni, 58
Shobogenzo (Dogen), 6
sitting (zazen)
authentic practice, 161–63
awareness in, ix–x, 5, 43
bottom-up practice, 35–39
challenges of, 104, 127, 162, 163
core beliefs and, 115
defined, 85
emotions and, 7, 8–9, 35, 36, 71
in everyday life, 159–61, 166–68
first rule of, 103–4
group nature of, 105
and not-thinking, 37–38
ordinary nature of, 131–32
physical nature of, x, 7, 36, 105,
    159
psychotherapy integrated, 143–54
purpose of, 46, 116–17, 121, 122
resistance and, 35, 43
rewards of, x, 7, 104–5, 116, 123,
    163
structure-building dimension,
    103–5
top-down practice, 25–33

traditional, 159, 162–63
uselessness of, 115–25
work practice in, 109–10
Socrates, 21
the soul, 60
stoicism, 71
Stolorow, Robert, 21–22, 77, 79, 90
Sung-Yüan's Person of Great Strength
    (koan), 50–54
Suzuki, S., 131

T
teacher/student relationships, 9–11,
    106, 129–33
teisho, defined, 176
"The Borderline Concept" (Stolorow
    and Brandchaft), 21
think not-thinking, 37–38
top-down practice, 25–29
transcendence/no transcendence,
    82–83
transference
defined, 177
described, 9–10
narcissistic, 15–19
neurosis, 131
Oedipal, 18
selfobject, 18–20, 105, 106
twinship selfobject, 105
transformation, x, xi, 150
true self, 66–72, 79, 82–83
twinship selfobject transference, 19,
    105

U
Uchiyama, K., 116, 124, 161–62
the Unborn, 88–90, 92–93, 117, 166
the unconscious, 88–93, 106–8, 119

V
van de Wetering, Janwillem, 8, 155
Vico, Giovanni, 14

W
Wash Your Bowl (koan), 125–27

Whalen, Philip, 94
What Shakes Your Tree? (koan),
    155–57
What was your original face before
    you were born? (koan), 66–67
Why has the man of great satori not
    cut the red thread? (koan), 54
Wittgenstein, Ludwig, 40–41, 53, 163
Wolf, Ernest, 78
work practice, 109–11
"A World without Substances or
    Essences" (Rorty), 68–69
Wu-men, 6
Wu-tsu's Buffalo Passes through the
    Window (koan), 119

Z
zazen (sitting). See sitting (zazen)
"Zen and Grammar" (Blyth), 53
Zen and the Brain (Austin), 56
Zen moths, 66, 74
Zen psychotherapy differences. See
    also psychoanalysis
  affect regulation development, 105
  consciousness states, 56
  difficult challenges, 102
  oneness experiences, 35

repetition, 108–9
selfobject experiences, 106
unconscious organizing principles,
    92, 101, 107–8
uncovered material handling, xi
Zen psychotherapy similarities. See
    also psychoanalysis
  affect regulation development, 103,
    105
  authentic practice controversy, 161
  authority relationships, 129–30
  awareness, 1
  bottom-up practice, 35–36
  core beliefs questioning, 36, 138–39
  determinism beliefs, 120
  difficult experiences, 127
    discipline and relationship, 163
    goal of, 82
  insight, 63
  mind modeling, 2
  relating patterns, 138–39
  resistance inquiry, 58
  suffering, approach to, 2
  unconscious organizing principles,
    90–91, 107–8

ABOUT THE AUTHOR

Barry Magid is a psychiatrist and psycho-analyst practicing in New York City. He completed his medical studies at the New Jersey College of Medicine in 1975, and currently serves as a faculty member and supervisor at the Institute for Contemporary Psychotherapy, and the Postgraduate Center for Mental Health, where he completed his psychoanalytic training in 1981. He is a Dharma heir of Charlotte Joko Beck, and the founding teacher of the Ordinary Mind Zendo in New York City. Magid has published numerous articles within the psychoanalytic field of self psychology and is the editor of *Freud's Case Studies: Self Psychological Perspectives* (Analytic Press, 1993) and *Father Louie: Photographs of Thomas Merton by Ralph Eugene Meatyard* (Timken, 1991).

In October 1996, Chartotte Joko Beck gave him permission to establish The Ordinary Mind Zendo as an affiliate of the San Diego Zen Center, and to serve as its Zen Teacher. He received Dharma transmission from Joko in1999. He is committed to the ongoing integration of the practices of psychodynamic psychotherapy and Zen.

Since 1989, he has also hand printed books at the Center for Books Arts in New York City, and has published limited editions of works by Wendell Berry, Guy Davenport, Mark Doty, Jonathan Greene, Jim Harrison, James Laughlin, Thomas Merton, Robert Stone, Charles Tomlinson, Jonathan Williams, William Carlos Williams, and others under the imprint of the Dim Gray Bar Press. His own translation of Diogenes Laertius' "Life of Zeno," was published by Larkspur Press in 1996.

He is married to the poet Sharon Dolin.

ABOUT WISDOM

Wisdom Publications, a not-for-profit publisher, is dedicated to preserving and transmitting important works from all the major Buddhist traditions as well as related East-West themes.

To learn more about Wisdom, or to browse our books on-line, visit our website at wisdompubs.org.

If you would like to receive our mail-order catalog, please write to:

Wisdom Publications
199 Elm Street
Somerville, Massachusetts 02144 USA
Telephone: (617) 776-7416 • Fax: (617) 776-7841
Email: sales@wisdompubs.org • www.wisdompubs.org

THE WISDOM TRUST

As a not-for-profit publisher, Wisdom Publications is dedicated to the publication of fine books for the benefit of all and is dependent upon the kindness and generosity of sponsors in order to be so. If you would like to make a donation to Wisdom, please do so through our Somerville office. If you would like to help sponsor the publication of a book, please write or email us for more information.

Thank you.

Wisdom Publications is a nonprofit 501(c)(3) organization affiliated with the Foundation for the Preservation of the Mahayana Tradition (FPMT).